D0330844

The Laws of Thermodynamics

An Anthology of Current Thought

Edited by Jennifer Viegas

The Rosen Publishing Group, Inc., New York

Published in 2006 by The Rosen Publishing Group, Inc.
29 East 21st Street, New York, NY 10010

Library of Congress Cataloging-in-Publication Data

The laws of thermodynamics: an anthology of current thought/
edited by Jennifer Viegas.—1st ed.
 p. cm.—(Contemporary discourse in the field of physics)
Includes bibliographical references.
ISBN 1-4042-0409-1 (library binding)
1. Thermodynamics—Popular works. I. Viegas, Jennifer. II. Series.

QC311.L3428 2006
536'.7—dc22

           2004029662

Manufactured in the United States of America

On the cover (clockwise from top right): Patterns of light on a
white surface; a colored macrophotograph of bubbles of steam in
boiling water; portrait of Sir Isaac Newton; liquid crystal.

CONTENTS

Introduction

Physics is the study of matter and energy, and how each interacts with the other. The basic terminology sometimes confuses people, but, in essence, physics is the science of everything. The stuff that makes up the universe is either matter or energy. If something else does exist that is neither matter nor energy, then physics would absorb the mysterious phenomenon, too. Physics seeks to find the underlying mechanics of matter and energy. Within physics lies a field of study that today is both literally and figuratively hot—thermodynamics.

Thermodynamics is the study of heat and its relation to other forms of energy. If you are new to the subject, then you might first think it is limited to heaters, air conditioners, electricity, and the like. Thermodynamics, however, affects most things in the universe, from the cells in your body to the explosive activity of the Sun, which fuels all life in our galaxy.

As you will soon read in the selections contained within this anthology, research concerning thermodynamics may one day lead to cures for diseases, better technologies, and cleaner energy sources, among other innovations. The more physicists learn about thermodynamics, the more apparent it becomes that innovations in this field have seemingly countless potential ways of improving our daily lives.

The first human observance of the power of thermodynamics might have happened over a Stone Age campfire. People may have placed a cooking vessel full of food or liquid over the fire and then fitted the container with a makeshift cover, such as a leaf. If enough steam built up, the leaf could have shot into the air and caused the awaiting diners to scratch their heads and wonder, "What just happened here?"

A similar bit of speculation occurred in the mid-1800s on a ship in the tropics. German scientist Julius Robert von Mayer (1814–1878) was serving as a doctor on the ship when he noticed something very peculiar. His patients from the tropics had blood in their veins that was redder than the blood he had seen in his northern climate patients. Varying rates of oxidation explained the differences, but the observation also inspired him to think about how the human body produces energy and gives off heat. The theorizing led to the earliest formulation of the first law of thermodynamics.

There are two main parts to the first law. The first part states that heat is energy, which is something that has the capacity to do work. For the Stone Age scenario, the heat under the cooking vessel had energy that transferred to liquid within the pot that moved the leaf. Heat, therefore, is not just a measurement of temperature. It is energy itself.

The second part of the first law of thermodynamics states that energy within a system is conserved. As an example, a popular comic strip features a character that forever puts all of his energy into kicking a football, but he always misses and falls flat on his back. The energy that he exerts is not transferred to the football. Instead, it is felt in the force of the impact when he hits the ground. Energy does not disappear. It simply spreads out or transfers to other matter.

French scientist Sadi Carnot, about whom you will read more later in this book, developed the second law of thermodynamics. The second law holds that a machine cannot be built that will convert thermal, or heat, energy into mechanical energy with complete efficiency. In other words, 100 percent of the energy will not do the desired work. You can feel the evidence for this principle if you touch the hood of an idling car or the back of a computer that is turned on. You likely will detect heat. The heat on the car hood serves no useful purpose. It is simply waste heat that wound up not contributing to the mechanical energy that runs the car.

This second law led to a concept that runs counter to mechanical energy, entropy. If mechanical energy is ordered, then entropy represents disorder. Rudolf Clausius, another German scientist from the mid-1800s, devoted much of his time to thinking about entropy. He came up with two fundamental ideas that greatly influenced physicists then and now. In a way, they represent the two laws of thermodynamics explained in a different manner. Clausius determined that the energy of the universe is constant and that the universe's entropy tends to a maximum, which means that disorder is always on the rise.

Entropy can be thought of in terms of probability. Molecules are more likely to become disordered than ordered. What are the chances that the sand on a beach will suddenly form itself into a sand castle? There is always a chance, but it is extremely slim. The chances are greater that the sand will disperse in a random fashion.

Experts in thermodynamics often refer to the first two laws, but there is also a third law of thermodynamics. Yet another German scientist from the mid-1800s, Hermann Nernst, created the third law. It states that an object's entropy goes to zero when the object's temperature reaches absolute zero. An object at absolute zero, therefore, is said to be an object in complete order because entropy's disorder is not present.

Absolute zero exists in theory rather than practice, because it has been impossible for scientists to completely remove all energy from an atomic structure. The wave properties that bind electrons and protons together form the observable object. If those properties are removed, then the location and the momentum of the particle change as you are trying to view it. The scientific description of this occurrence is called the uncertainty principle, a theory that was developed in 1927 by Werner Heisenberg.

Heisenberg, Albert Einstein, and other prominent twentieth-century physicists opened up a completely new world of physics with quantum mechanics, which looks at energy and matter, but at their smallest units of construction. The photons that make up light and the protons and electrons that make up atomic structures are today the focus of much study. When quantum mechanics meets thermodynamics, the resulting marriage is about as explosive as a nuclear bomb.

You will detect some of that explosiveness in the following articles. Thermodynamics today is in a transitional phase, just as we are all dependent on technologies that we know will change in the coming years. Scientists are holding on to the old laws of the past, but they are also coming up with new data that might challenge those laws in the future.

Humans, computers, and even Earth itself can be thought of as systems. Could a system in the future operate perpetually with no disorder and no need for fuel? Do quantum particles transfer their energies from one state to another in dimensions that might suggest universes parallel to our own? Advances in thermodynamics may very well answer these astounding questions and more in your lifetime. But we are getting ahead of ourselves. The selections included here represent the present state of thermodynamics. They also hint at what the future might bring. Today's theories, like your vision for your own future, may represent tomorrow's realities. —JV

1

Thermodynamics, Entropy, and Quantum Mechanics

Scientists refer to the degree of disorder or uncertainty in a system as entropy. Rudolf Clausius developed the concept in the mid-nineteenth century, when thermodynamics was gaining steam, so to speak, thanks to steam and other engine technologies. Clausius wondered why mechanical engines produced waste heat, and why not all of the produced heat could be converted back into mechanical energy. It seemed as if a system went from order to disorder.

The theory can apply to all things in the universe, even humans, other animals, and plants. In our youth, our cells tend to function with greater precision than they do over a period of a lifetime, due to mutations that can lead to imperfections. Engines also wear out, but even a new car or computer does not operate with complete efficiency, in part due to entropic forces.

Brandeis University researchers have discovered that entropy may be a case of "is the glass half full or half empty?" As described in this *article, scientist Seth Fraden and his colleagues found that entropic forces also produce seemingly opposite depletion forces that may counter the negative effects associated with entropy. This work describes what goes on at the microscopic level, where cells and particles of different shapes, such as spheres and rods, interact with each other. The research is very promising, as it might not only improve machine technologies, but it could also lead to medical breakthroughs for cellular diseases, such as sickle cell anemia.* —JV

"Another Face of Entropy: Particles Self-Organize to Make Room for Randomness"
by Peter Weiss
Science News, August 15, 1998

There's a flip side to the doom and gloom of entropy. The steady march to disorder is not all degradation and the ultimate, bland sameness found so depressing by thinkers from philosopher Bertrand Russell to novelist Thomas Pynchon.

Entropy measures the amount of disorder in any patch of the universe, be it the dust, gas, stars, and planets of a galaxy, a belching steam engine, or the cells of a living organism. The laws of thermodynamics require that entropy must always increase. Rudolf Clausius, the 19th century German physicist, imagined that the relentless increase of entropy would ultimately degrade the universe to a disordered, stagnant confusion—a fate he called the heat-death.

As Russell sadly put it, "all the labors of the ages, all the devotion, all the inspiration, all the noonday brightness of human genius, are destined to extinction." And, Pynchon's character Callisto in the story "Entropy," bemoaned a heat-death of culture as well, "in which ideas, like heat-energy, would no longer be transferred."

Scientists, however, are discovering with apparent glee how often the road to disorder is paved with a little useful order. "Even though it's been known for a long time that entropy can produce order, it's still not fully realized how general that phenomenon is and how rich in potential," says Seth Fraden of Brandeis University in Waltham, Mass.

That potential holds in particular for a submerged realm of objects that are much bigger than atoms but too small to be seen without a microscope. There, remarkable feats of self-assembly take place. Such processes can create intricate molecular structures that, despite appearances, represent an increase of entropy over their ingredients.

It's a realm of special importance to humankind because it encompasses the contents of biological cells. In optics, it's the arena where researchers strive to make the photonic crystals that have been touted as the silicon of future, light-based computing. It's also where scientists grapple with problems of protein crystallization—a vital step toward understanding the functions of many new-found genes.

Although scientists have known since at least the 1940s that entropy can act as an unseen hand to create order, only in the last few years have they begun to suspect—and to demonstrate—how elaborate its handiwork can be. They have found that simply blending microscopic particles of different shapes or sizes in liquids sometimes causes crystalline structures of remarkable complexity to appear. The aimless interactions of the particles creates these structures, even while maximizing entropy as thermodynamics demands.

In entropy's most virtuoso laboratory performance to date, Fraden and his colleagues at Brandeis University blended plastic spheres and rods in water. The spheres, each no larger than a micron in diameter, were combined with micron-long rods—actually genetically engineered viruses—about 10 nanometers in diameter.

In experiments reported in the May 28 NATURE, the suspended mixtures spontaneously solidified into two types of highly ordered, complex, permanent structures. One is a cake in which layers of vertical rods alternate with a thin frosting of balls—a stacked, or lamellar, arrangement. This pattern reflects the arrangement of phospholipids in cell membranes and the alignment of soap molecules in the surfaces of bubbles.

The other structure, known as columnar, features a regular, crystal lattice of vertical columns of clustered spheres embedded in a horizontal sea of rods all pointing roughly the same way.

Polymers used as glues and soaps commonly take on such structure, a phenomenon that materials scientists have long attributed to an incompatibility between the ends of the polymer molecules. The rods used by Fraden and his colleagues, however, don't have antagonistic ends.

Seeing a glue-like or soap-like structure built purely by entropic forces was "shocking," he says. Other, less durable patterns also emerged, including ropes with lamellar order and chains of rod packets interspersed with spheres.

A new, unpublished study by Arjun Yodh and his colleagues at the University of Pennsylvania in Philadelphia may cast light on how such elaborate structures form.

Since the early 1990s, Yodh's lab has been probing how the organizing influences of entropy arise, how strong they are, and how to control them. In a series of papers dating to early 1994, the researchers have described mixing small beads with large spheres— typically in proportions of thousands of small spheres less than 100 nanometers in diameter for each large sphere, which is 500 or so nanometers across. As the scientists watch, the bigger ones are pushed by their smaller neighbors against the hard, flat walls of containers, where they assemble into crystals.

In other experiments detailed in the January 12 PHYSICAL REVIEW LETTERS, the team observed big balls being forced against the most curved sections of the inner walls of pear-shaped, rigid vessels.

A few simple principles seem to explain where the large spheres go, according to Yodh and other scientists. First, the entropy of the small balls reaches its peak when they have the most room in which to move. Second, the large balls hog more room than just the actual volume that they occupy. Both large balls and walls, by their very presence, create thin regions along their surfaces where some part of each small ball cannot go.

For instance, a small ball's center must stay at least one small-ball radius away from those surfaces. However, those restrictive regions can overlap and cancel each other out where a big ball and a wall or another ball touch. The overlap is even greater at concave walls. By herding the big balls against walls or each other via random collisions, the small balls regain some unfettered volume and raise their entropy.

Of course, the entropy of the big balls drops as they form neat clusters, but calculations show that the overall entropy still goes up, the experimenters say.

In essence, entropy creates an attractive force that is also called a depletion, or excluded-volume, force. The strength of this force, first predicted in 1958 by Japanese physicists Sho Asakura and Fumio Oosawa of Nagoya University, depends on the ratio of small to large spheres and their relative sizes. John Y. Walz of Yale University, a researcher who has measured the minuscule force, describes it as "less than the weight of a single red blood cell in water."

In Yodh's new study, the experimenters again mixed small and large balls. They then tracked the separation of pairs of large spheres to determine the force between them. John Crocker reported the new data in March at a meeting of the American Physical Society in Los Angeles.

At modest concentrations of small spheres, the force was attractive, as expected, decreasing with distance between the spheres. But, at high concentrations of little balls, the force flip-flopped repeatedly, changing from attractive at the closest separation, to repulsive further out, then back to attractive, and so on.

Theorists had predicted this effect, but Yodh's team is the first to measure it between two spheres. Two years ago, Walz and Amber Sharma, also of Yale, saw the same effect while measuring the force between a sphere and a wall. Due to alternating attraction and repulsion, large spheres could become trapped in layers at successive distances from each other.

These entropic forces become significant at scales of, roughly, a few tens of nanometers to a couple of microns. For entropic ordering to take place, particles must constantly jostle each other and be light enough to be randomly agitated by fluid molecules, making gravity negligible. Proteins, DNA, and other macro-molecules that crowd a cell's cytoplasm fit the bill, some researchers say.

Most biology researchers have paid no heed to entropic forces because traditional biochemistry focuses on reactions in dilute solutions, away from the cellular "background," says Allen P. Minton, a physical chemist at the National Institutes of Health in Bethesda, Md.

In the late 1970s, however, he and his colleague Philip D. Ross showed how excluded-volume forces could account for an unexplained clumping of sickle-cell hemoglobin in the presence of other proteins that play the role of the small spheres in entropy experiments.

A few years later, Minton and Steven B. Zimmerman, also at NIH, tied entropic forces to the clustering of DNA in cells lacking a nucleus. Currently, Minton is probing the role such forces might play in the binding of proteins to cell membranes and in the assembly of the cell's structural scaffold of protein filaments known as microtubules.

Working with Yodh's group, Dennis E. Discher, a biophysicist at the University of Pennsylvania, is examining whether depletion forces are partly responsible for clumping of blood cells in the body when circulation is blocked. Also, extending Yodh's work to thinner-walled containers, much more like actual cells, Discher hopes to measure the force that can be exerted by a large sphere pushed outward by depletion forces. He speculates that it may be such entropic forces that eject the nucleus from red blood cells before they enter the bloodstream.

"There is a lot of evidence that [entropic forces are] a very widespread and important phenomenon in biological systems," says Minton, a self-proclaimed missionary for the idea. It may be catching on, he adds, given the rising number of invitations he has been receiving to speak and write review papers on "macromolecular crowding," as the phenomenon is known in biology.

In several ways, industry has already recognized the utility of entropic ordering—and also dealt with its down side. In the 1940s, Nobel laureate Lars Onsager predicted a phase transition due to entropic forces. Thirty years later, chemists achieved that phase change among polymer molecules, inducing them to bind together to form ultra-strong fibers such as Kevlar.

In the 1980s, unexpected findings by paint makers fueled a resurgence of interest in entropic ordering.

Polymers that had been added to paint to make it flow smoothly were instead causing clumping. The culprit: excluded-volume forces.

The growing appreciation of entropy's penchant for order has unleashed a renewed drive to put it to practical use. Yodh and physicist David Pine of the University of California, Santa Barbara are each trying to exploit entropy to make photonic crystals, which are expected to lead to better microlasers and possibly all-optical computer circuits that are smaller, faster, and create less heat than conventional electronics.

Each is basing his research on their joint discovery that by cutting grooves in the walls of the container to which the spheres adhere, scientists can direct where entropic forces herd large spheres. That finding was detailed in a Sept. 19, 1996 NATURE paper with Anthony D. Dinsmore, now at the Naval Research Laboratory in Washington, D.C.

Now they plan to use the entropy-ordered spheres as seeds for photonic crystals designed so that the walls of their inner pores reflect light in all directions.

Large photonic crystals suitable for manipulating long wavelengths of light, such as microwaves, already exist. Yodh and Pine, however, each intend to create crystals that can handle infrared or visible light, which promise to be far more useful but are difficult to make because they require such fine internal structure.

Nonetheless, Pine believes he is only months away from success. He is using grooves to align spheres of oil suspended in a fluid. He next fills the space around the globules with ceramic materials that tend to scatter light in all directions. When the ceramic hardens, Pine clears out the liquids to leave the desired crystal behind.

Yodh is also using grooves, but he applies beads of similar light-dispersing materials directly to create the crystal. It's a tough challenge because the material is so heavy that gravity enters the equation.

Success for his group might depend on escaping gravity, which is what the researchers intend to do. NASA has awarded them a grant for microgravity experiments on the space shuttle, although a date has not yet been set, Yodh says.

A better understanding of entropic forces might also transform the "black art" of protein crystallization into a reliable process with a firmer scientific footing, Fraden says.

He pledges to devote the next couple of years to that task. He predicts that as scientists attempt to learn what the genes described by the Human Genome Project do, they will reach a bottleneck because their ability to crystallize proteins is limited. Crystals are required to determine the three-dimensional structure of proteins, which give clues to their function.

In the Sept. 26, 1997 SCIENCE, researchers reported computer simulations showing that entropic forces could allow proteins to crystallize readily. In their models, adding polymer particles to a protein suspension induces the formation of dense droplets that act as seeds for crystal formation, say Daan Frenkel and Pieter Rein ten Wolde of the FOM Institute for Atomic and Molecular Physics in Amsterdam.

Also swept up in the revival is Alice P. Gast at Stanford University, whose doctoral thesis 13 years ago quantified the entropy-induced clumping that baffled paint manufacturers. After turning her attention to other things, she is now returning to entropic forces—this time as a way to grow two-dimensional protein crystals.

Experiments on entropy-driven ordering have also caught the eye of physicist Adam J. Simon at Merck & Co., a pharmaceutical firm in West Point, Pa. "If these entropic or depletion forces are playing a role in cellular processes, then there is potential application in the field of drug delivery," he says.

Although excited by new findings and applications, even scientists who have studied depletion forces for years admit that entropy's orderly alter ego can befuddle their intuition. But once you have seen entropy tidy up, the researchers say, you start noticing its touches everywhere.

Quantum mechanics is a somewhat new field of scientific study. Einstein developed many of its fundamental principles in the 1900s, well after the laws of thermodynamics had first been formulated. Progress since then has been somewhat slow, as researchers are limited by equipment and materials, since the quantum world is not visible to the naked eye.

In this paper, which was published in a peer-reviewed journal, the team of researchers carefully speculates about the possibilities of quantum engines within the accepted framework of accepted thermodynamic laws and theory. To challenge a physics gold standard like the idealized Carnot engine requires caution and tact, both of which are exercised here.

A quantum designed engine can operate one cycle, or a set number of cycles, within a fixed time frame. A theory behind Carnot's engine, however, states that each cycle is infinitely long. In the twentieth century, scientists did not have the technology to create things like doped semiconductors, which can maximize or minimize heat transfer on the atomic scale. It will be interesting to see whether any of the old, accepted laws will be altered based on findings from quantum mechanic analysis. —JV

"Entropy and Temperature of a Quantum Carnot Engine"
by Carl M. Bender, Dorje C. Brody, and
Bernhard K. Meister
Proceedings of the Royal Society: Mathematical, Physical and Engineering Sciences, June 8, 2002

It is possible to extract work from a quantum-mechanical system whose dynamics is governed by a time-dependent cyclic Hamiltonian. An *energy bath* is required to operate such a quantum engine in place of the heat bath used to run a conventional classical thermodynamic heat engine. The effect of the energy bath is to maintain the expectation value of the system Hamiltonian during an isoenergetic expansion. It is shown that the existence of such a bath leads to equilibrium quantum states that maximise the von Neumann entropy. Quantum analogues of certain thermodynamic relations are obtained that allow one to define the temperature of the energy bath.

A classical thermodynamic heat engine converts heat energy into mechanical work by using a classical mechanical system in which a gas expands and pushes a piston in a cylinder. Such a heat engine obtains its energy from a high-temperature heat reservoir. Some of the energy taken from this reservoir is converted to mechanical work. A heat engine is not perfectly efficient, so some of the energy taken from the heat reservoir is not converted to mechanical energy, but rather is transferred to a low-temperature reservoir [1].

A classical heat engine running between a high-temperature reservoir and a low-temperature reservoir achieves maximum efficiency if it is reversible. While it is impossible to construct a working heat engine that is perfectly reversible, in the early 19th century Carnot proposed mathematical model of an ideal heat engine that is not only reversible but also cyclic [2]. The Carnot engine consists of a cylinder of ideal gas that is alternately placed in thermal contact with high-temperature and low-temperature heat reservoirs whose temperatures are T_H and T_C, respectively.

Instead of a classical system of gas, we consider here a quantum-mechanical system consisting of a single particle in contact with a reservoir. The system is described by a time-dependent cyclic Hamiltonian. The statistical ensemble of many such identically-prepared systems is characterised by a density matrix. We assume that the system interacts weakly with its environment. It is known that it is possible to extract work from such a system [3, 4]. In particular, if the evolution of the density matrix is reversible, then we can construct a quantum-mechanical Carnot engine [5]. The purpose of the present paper is to investigate the properties of quantum Carnot engine. This is of importance because it improves our understanding of the relationship between thermodynamics and quantum mechanics, an area of considerable interest in quantum theory [6].

This paper is organised as follows: First, we explain the concept of a quantum engine by generalising the two-state model considered in [5] to an infinite-state square-well model and derive equations of states for isoenergetic and adiabatic processes. These results lead naturally to the quantum analogue of the Clausius equality for a reversible cycle. We show that, unlike the result in classical thermodynamics, the Clausius relation obtained here is not based on the change of entropy. We then introduce the von Neumann entropy and obtain the maximum entropy state subject to isoenergetic requirements. We demonstrate that the maximum von Neumann entropy is consistent with the thermodynamic definition of entropy. As a consequence, we are able to determine the temperature of the energy bath directly from two of the diagonal components of the density matrix. We conclude by discussing several open problems.

We can construct a simple quantum engine using a single particle of mass m confined to an infinite one-dimensional square-well potential whose volume is V (in one-dimension the volume is just the width of the well). For any fixed V it is easy to solve the time independent Schrödinger equation to determine the energy spectrum of the system:

$$E_n(V) = \frac{\pi^2 \hbar^2 n^2}{2m V^2} . \tag{1}$$

We assume that the width of the well initially is $V = V_1$ and that the initial energy of the system is a fixed constant E_H. The initial state $\psi(x)$ of the system is a linear combination $\psi(x) = \Sigma a_n \Phi_n(x)$ of the energy eigenstates $\Phi_n(x)$. Thus,

$$\sum_{n=1}^{\infty} p_n E_n(V_1) = E_H , \tag{2}$$

where $p_n = |a_n|^2.$ Note that E_H is bounded below by $E_H \geq E_1(V_1)$.

Starting with the above initial configuration, we define a quantum cycle as follows: First, the well expands *isoenergetically*; that is, the width of the well increases infinitely slowly while the system is kept in contact with an energy bath. Note that the quantum adiabatic theorem [7] states that if the system were isolated during such an expansion, the system would remain in its initial state; That is, the absolute values of the expansion coefficients $|a_n|$ would remain constant. Thus, if the system were isolated, the energy of the system (the expectation value of the Hamiltonian) would decrease like V^{-2}. However, during this expansion, we simultaneously pump energy into the system in order to compensate this decrease of the energy. Thus, the well, which can be viewed as a one-dimensional piston, expands in such a way that the expectation value of the Hamiltonian is held constant by exciting higher energy states. During such an isoenergetic expansion, mechanical work is done by the force (one-dimensional pressure) P on the walls of the well. Note that the contribution to this force from the nth energy eigenstate is $f_n = \pi^2 \hbar^2 n^2 / (mV^3)$. Hence the force P is given by the expectation value $P = \Sigma p_n f_n$. Using the relation $f_n = 2E_n/V$ and Eq. (2), we obtain the equation of state during an isoenergetic process:

$$PV = 2E_H . \tag{3}$$

This result is identical to the corresponding equation of state for an isothermal process of a classical ideal gas, if we make the identification $2E_H \longleftrightarrow kT_H$. Note that the expansion coefficients a_n of the wave function change as a function of the width V while the well expands isoenergetically from V_1 to V_2.

Second, the system expands *adiabatically*. During an adiabatic process the eigenstates $\phi_n(x)$ change as a function of V, but the values $|a_n|$ remain constant. Therefore, the expectation value of the Hamiltonian

$E = \Sigma p_n E_n(V)$ decreases during the process because each E_n decreases with increasing V while all p_n are kept fixed. The force P in this case is determined by differentiating the energy E with respect to V. Thus, the equation of state during an adiabatic process for the square-well potential is

$$PV^{3} = 2V_2^2 E_H ,\qquad (4)$$

which is a quantum analogue of the corresponding equation for a classical ideal gas. The system expands adiabatically until its volume reaches $V = V_3$. At this point the expectation of the Hamiltonian decreases to E_C. Because the squared coefficients p_n of the wave function remain constant during an adiabatic process, the value of E_C is given by $E_C = (V_2^2/V_3^2)E_H$.

Following the adiabatic expansion, the system is compressed isoenergetically until $V = V_4$, with the expectation value of the Hamiltonian fixed at E_C, and finally it is compressed adiabatically until the width of the system returns to its initial value $V = V_1$. This cycle is reversible, and we find that the efficiency of the quantum engine is given by

$$\eta = 1 - \frac{E_C}{E_H} ,\qquad (5)$$

a formula analogous to the classical thermodynamic result $\eta = 1 - T_C/T_H$ of Carnot.

We have demonstrated above an example of a quantum system with a time-dependent Hamiltonian from which work can be extracted. The key concept introduced here is an *energy bath* that maintains the expectation value of the Hamiltonian. This idea can be developed further to establish the quantum counterparts of the classical thermodynamic relations. To begin with, let us first consider the theorem of Clausius.

During an isoenergetic expansion, the amount of energy transferred to the system to maintain the expectation of the Hamiltonian is determined by the integral

$$Q_H = \int_{V_1}^{V_2} dV\, P(V) = 2E_H \ln(V_2/V_1), \qquad (6)$$

where $P(V)$ is given by (3). An essentially identical formula was derived by Carnot [2] from studying the system of a classical gas. The amount of energy absorbed during an isoenergetic compression can be determined similarly with the result $Q_C = -2E_C \ln(V_3/V_4)$. Thus, for a closed, reversible cycle we obtain the quantum Clausius equality

$$\frac{Q_H}{E_H} + \frac{Q_C}{E_C} = 0, \qquad (7)$$

because $V_2/V_1 = V_3/V_4$ for a closed cycle.

In classical thermodynamics the Clausius equality states that the total change $\oint dS$ of entropy in a reversible cycle is zero, where the differential of entropy $dS = dQ/T$ is the ratio of the absorbed heat and the bath temperature. Therefore, the relation (7) suggests that in quantum mechanics the entropy change

in an isoenergetic process might be given by dQ/E, the ratio of the absorbed energy to the bath energy. However, as we show below, this quantity does not determine the amount of entropy change, and hence the quantum Clausius relation is not a condition for entropy. Instead, it merely implies that the total energy absorbed, for given bath energies, must vanish in a reversible cycle. If the cycle is irreversible, then we have $\oint dQ/E < 0$.

To understand the change of entropy in a quantum Carnot cycle we consider the von Neumann entropy

$$S = -\sum_{n=1}^{\infty} p_n \ln(p_n) \qquad (8)$$

associated with the density matrix $\rho_{mn} = p_n \delta_{mn}$ expressed in terms of the energy eigenstates. Let us first consider the isoenergetic process and introduce a scaling parameter λ such that $V = \lambda V_1$. Then, during an isoenergetic process the probability p_n that the system is in the nth eigenstate changes in λ, subject to the constraints

$$\sum_{n=1}^{\infty} p_n = 1 \quad \text{and} \quad \sum_{n=1}^{\infty} n^2 p_n = \lambda^2 , \qquad (9)$$

where we have chosen units in which $\pi^2 \hbar^2/(2m) = 1$ and taken the initial condition $E_H = E_1(V_1)$. There are infinitely many combinations of p_n satisfying these constraints, each of which determines the entropy. Hence, quantum mechanically it appears that any one of such states is allowed in an isoenergetic process. However, there is a unique density matrix that satisfies the thermodynamic requirement of the change of entropy, and this is the state that maximises the von Neumann entropy.

To show this, we must determine the density matrix that maximises the entropy subject to the constraints (9) and then obtain the associated entropy S. We can perform this maximisation directly without using Lagrange multipliers. The two constraints in (9) imply that two of the diagonal components, say p_k and p_l, of the density matrix are determined. Therefore, if we differentiate the constraints (9) with respect to p_n, we find that

$$\frac{\partial p_k}{\partial p_n} + \frac{\partial p_l}{\partial p_n} = -1 \quad \text{and} \quad k^2 \frac{\partial p_k}{\partial p_n} + l^2 \frac{\partial p_l}{\partial p_n} = -n^2.$$

Solving these linear equations, we obtain

$$\frac{\partial p_k}{\partial p_n} = -\frac{n^2 - l^2}{k^2 - l^2} \quad \text{and} \quad \frac{\partial p_l}{\partial p_n} = -\frac{n^2 - k^2}{l^2 - k^2} \tag{10}$$

for all $k, l \neq n$. Substituting these expressions into $\partial S / \partial p_n = 0$ and solving for p_n, we get

$$p_n = p_l \left(\frac{p_k}{p_l}\right)^{(n^2 - l^2)/(k^2 - l^2)}, \tag{11}$$

which is also valid for any choice of $k \neq l$.

Given the maximum entropy state (11), we can now reexpress the constraints in the form

$$\lambda^2 \sum_{n=1}^{\infty} \alpha^{n^2} = \sum_{n=1}^{\infty} n^2 \alpha^{n^2}, \tag{12}$$

where we have defined $\alpha = (p_k/p_1)^{1/(k^2-l^2)}$. This is obtained by substituting (11) in (9), solving for p_1, and equating the resulting expressions. Similarly, using the parameter α, the state represented in (11) can be expressed as

$$p_n = \frac{\alpha^{n^2}}{\sum_{m=1}^{\infty} \alpha^{m^2}}. \tag{13}$$

Therefore, the corresponding von Neumann entropy is

$$S = (l^2 - \lambda^2) \ln \alpha - \ln p_1. \tag{14}$$

This is independent of l because of the identity $p_k \alpha^{-k^2} = p_l \alpha^{-l^2}$. Thus, given the width scale $\lambda = V/V_1$ of the potential well, the relation (12) determines the value of α, from which we can determine both p_n and S as functions of the single length scale parameter λ.

We can now analyse the entropy associated with the isoenergetic process. We show first that the change of entropy associated with (14) does not agree with the quantity dQ/E. To verify this, we need only determine the asymptotic behaviour of S for large values of λ, that is, large energies. The reason is that, while different definitions of entropy change ΔS can give qualitatively different behaviours for low energies, they must agree in the high-energy limit to be consistent. In particular, because the value of S in (14) is independent of the choices of k and l, we can set $k = 2$ and $l = 1$ without loss of generality. Then, asymptotically we have $p_1 \sim p_2$ for large λ. Furthermore, the maximum entropy state

$\{p_n\}$ satisfies $p_k > p_l$ for all $k < l$. Therefore, $\alpha \sim 1$ and for large values of λ we use the asymptotic relation

$$\sum_{n=1}^{\infty} (1-\epsilon)^{n^2} \sim \frac{\sqrt{\pi}}{2\sqrt{\epsilon}} - \frac{1}{2} \ (\epsilon \to 0^+) \qquad (15)$$

to determine the entropy change. The result gives $\Delta S \sim \ln \lambda$ when the width changes from V_1 to $V = \lambda V_1$. On the other hand, from (6) we deduce that $dQ/E = 2 \ln \lambda$ for any value of $\lambda \geq 1$. Because entropy is defined up to an additive but not a multiplicative constant, we see that the two quantities are not equivalent even in the asymptotic regime.

Next, we show that the maximum von Neumann entropy (14) is consistent with thermodynamic consider-ations. Recall that an isoenergetic process must proceed infinitely slowly in order that the energy bath at any point during the process be in thermal equilibrium. Thus, this process requires an infinite amount of time to be realized. Then from the principles of statistical mechanics [8] we deduce that the temperature of the bath is given by $T = -1/\ln \alpha$ because of Eq. (13). On the other hand, temperature is given in thermodynamics by the formula

$$\frac{1}{T} = \frac{dS}{dQ}, \qquad (16)$$

where $dQ = PdV$. In the present consideration we have $dQ = 2\lambda d\lambda$ from the equation of state (3), while from (14) we find that $dS/d\lambda = -2\lambda \ln \alpha$. Therefore, the thermodynamic definition of temperature in (16) gives

$$T = -1/(\ln \alpha), \qquad (17)$$

which agrees with the statistical mechanical consideration above. We conclude that the maximum von Neumann entropy determines the density matrix of the system in an isoenergetic process. Furthermore, the temperature of the energy bath can be obtained from (17), where α is determined by any two diagonal components p_k, p_l of the density matrix. In particular, the temperature of the bath changes continuously in λ during an isoenergetic process, even though the energy is held fixed.

We now consider the adiabatic process. In this case, there is no net energy absorbed by the system, so the thermodynamic entropy remains constant. On the other hand, because the diagonal components p_n of the density matrix are constant during an adiabatic process, the von Neumann entropy (8) also remains constant, in agreement with the thermodynamic consideration.

These results can be expressed by the phase diagram in the entropy-volume plane, as shown in Fig. 1 [in the original article]. The diagram shows that the thermodynamic constraint $V_2/V_1 = V_3/V_4$ is satisfied by the maximum von Neumann entropy. Thus, we emphasise that the quantum state corresponding to the maximum von Neumann entropy, as obtained by microscopic analysis, is entirely consistent with the thermodynamic equations of states (3) and (4).

In the analysis above we have considered only the square-well potential model, which can be interpreted as the quantum analogue of the classical ideal gas. A natural extension of this work would be to consider other Hamiltonians. For example, for a harmonic potential whose energy eigenvalues are $E_n = (n + 1/2)\hbar\omega$, a dimensional argument shows that the characteristic length scale is given by $1/\sqrt{\omega}$. Therefore, the equations of states for the harmonic potential become identical to those for the square-well potential, although the volume dependence of the entropy is different from (14). For other Hamiltonians, however, the equations of states are not in general identical to those obtained here, and it would be interesting to find explicit examples of other models exhibiting nonideal behaviours.

Another important issue is to understand whether there is any role played by the geometric phases, a concept that does not have an analogue in the classical Carnot cycle. Although the quantum Carnot engine is indeed cyclic in terms of p_n, the coefficients a_n of the wave function inevitably pick up geometric phases as the system goes through a cycle. Therefore, strictly speaking, the wave function is not cyclic in the quantum Carnot cycle. The question then is whether there is any physically observable evidence of the geometric phase in the present context.

Finally, another interesting idea that should be studied is the possibility of constructing a *cyclic* quantum engine (or a quantum refrigerator by reversing the cycle) that requires only a finite amount of time to complete a cycle. Note that each cycle of a classical Carnot engine is infinitely long. However, in quantum mechanics, it is known, for example, that by choosing a specific form of time dependent Hamiltonians, it is possible to construct a quantum-mechanical cycle in an essentially arbitrary short time scale [9]. It would be of interest to determine if such an idea can be applied to

33

create a finite-time Carnot engine, or whether such dynamics would be incompatible with the requirement of maximising the von Neumann entropy.

1. M. Planck, *Treatise on Thermodynamics* (Longmans, Green and Co., Ltd., London 1927).
2. S. Carnot, *Réflexions sur la Puissance Motrice du Feu et sur les Machines Propres a Développer Cette Puissance* (Chez Bachelier, Paris 1824).
3. E. Geva and R. Kosloff, Phys. Rev. E **49**, 3903 (1994); R. Kosloff, E. Geva and J. M. Gordon, J. App. Phys. 87, 8093 (2000).
4. A. E. Allahverdyan and Th. M. Nieuwenhuizen, Phys. Rev. Lett. **85**, 1799 (2000).
5. C. M. Bender, D. C. Brody and B. K. Meister, J. Phys. A **33**, 4427 (2000).
6. H. S. Leff and A. F. Rex (eds.) *Maxwell's Demon, Entropy, Information, Computing* (Adam Hilger, Bristol 1990).
7. M. Born and V. Fock, Zeits. f. Physik **51**, 165 (1928).
8. E. Schrödinger, *Statistical Thermodynamics* (Cambridge University Press, Cambridge 1952).
9. B. Mielnik, J. Math. Phys. **27**, 2290 (1986).

Reprinted with permission from "Entropy and Temperature of a Quantum Carnot Engine," by Bender, Carl M., Dorje C. Brody, and Bernhard K. Meister, *Proceedings of the Royal Society: Mathematical, Physical and Engineering Sciences*, Volume 458, Number 2022, June 8, 2002, pp. 1519–1526. © 2002 The Royal Society.

Quantum mechanics is sometimes called wave mechanics because it refers to the wave properties of elementary particles. Research suggests that in the years to come, the laws of thermodynamics together with quantum principles will lead to smaller and much more efficient engines. "Quantum Engine Blasts Past High Gear" examines one such theory proposed by physicist Marlan Scully of Texas A&M University.

While Marlan Scully's engine exists primarily in theory, history reveals that comparable ideas and theoretical studies inspire the next generation's technology. Science-fiction books from the early 1900s onward often describe flying machines and spacecraft that are similar to those that actually were produced later. It is therefore possible that Scully's quantum engine will one day find itself in a future automobile, heat engine, or other commercial application.

The end of the article mentions the Carnot cycle. Sadi Carnot was a French scientist who was very concerned about France's economy after Napoléon's fall in 1815. At the age of twenty-eight, he began to intensely study heat engines and determined the maximum known efficiency of a real machine. Carnot died of cholera at the age of thirty-six, but his Carnot theorem is still a gold standard for thermodynamics. —JV

"Quantum Engine Blasts Past High Gear"
by David Voss
Science, January 18, 2002

All engines, whether the colossal thrusters on the space shuttle or the gasoline-fired power plant under the hood of your car, have to obey the laws of thermodynamics. Among other things, the laws set clear limits on the engines' efficiency: how much work they can squeeze from a given energy input. But take those classical axioms and add quantum mechanics, and unusual things can happen. Recently, Marlan Scully, a physicist at Texas A&M University, College Station, has discovered that in the quantum world, you can sometimes reap more horsepower than you'd expect.

Scully found that in theory he could take the hot exhaust from one kind of heat engine and drive a laser with it. Lasers work by storing energy in the internal quantum energy states of atoms or molecules and then releasing the energy in the form of photons. But heat engines generally ignore the internal states and instead harness the thermal motions of atoms and molecules in the "working fluid" (for example, the hot gas made by burning gasoline) as it expands and moves pistons to turn a crankshaft. The twist in Scully's scheme is to trade energy between the external and internal states of the atoms in a carefully choreographed way so as to squeeze a few more drops of work out of the engine.

In a paper accepted for publication in *Physical Review Letters*, Scully applies the concept to a type of heat engine called the Otto cycle, a cousin to the common car engine. Scully considers an idealized version of this engine without the exploding gasoline, instead just considering what happens as gas is compressed, is heated, does work, and is cooled again.

In his scheme, Scully takes the still-hot gas in the expanded piston chamber and routes it into a laser cavity, where the internal quantum states of the gas molecules come into play. The hot exhaust that would normally just be shoved out the door gets used to create more useful work by means of the laser emission. As a result, the total energy out is more than you'd expect from classical thermodynamic analysis of an "ideal" Otto cycle engine.

"I think it's a nice paper, very fun, and it's potentially useful," says Seth Lloyd, a physicist at the Massachusetts Institute of Technology. After hearing Scully give a talk about the concept, Lloyd dubbed the theoretical gadget a "quantum afterburner" by analogy to the devices that squeeze extra thrust out of the exhaust from a jet engine. "It takes advantage of a source of energy that hasn't been taken advantage of before," Lloyd says. After all, "the steam engine wasn't very useful until James Watt came along and made it more efficient. He didn't invent the steam engine, but he figured out how to control it."

Scully acknowledges that his analysis is controversial. But he says that doubters who once attacked him for flirting with perpetual motion have come around. "In thermodynamics, the devil is in the details, but so are the angels," he says. "You have to look at a specific physical system [such as the engine] and not just abstract thermodynamic calculations." Ronnie Kosloff, a theoretical chemist at Hebrew University in Jerusalem, agrees that Scully's concept is on solid ground: "It is consistent with all the laws of thermodynamics."

To check that his equations were on the up-and-up, Scully recently put his quantum afterburner to the ultimate theoretical test: hooking it up to an engine running at maximal efficiency. Until then, he had applied it only to the Otto cycle engine, which runs less efficiently than thermodynamics allows. But when Scully probed how well such a device would work with the ideal Carnot cycle, the gold standard of thermodynamic machines, the quantum afterburner couldn't squeeze out any extra energy—proof, Scully says, that his theoretical device is playing by the rules.

Reprinted with permission from Voss, David, "Quantum Engine Blasts Past High Gear," *Science* 295: 425 (2002). © 2002 AAAS.

Any new product must undergo tests to see that it meets certain standards before manufacturers place it on the market. New medicines and food products, for example, must pass FDA standards. Scientists operate within a similar restrictive framework, even when they formulate theories. For an idea to gain widespread acceptance among academics, it must follow established laws.

The first and second laws of thermodynamics are nicely summarized in this article, which was written for a lay audience consisting of people who are interested in science but who are not necessarily scientists themselves. Physicists who study quantum mechanics sometimes find that their theories fall outside of accepted ideologies. Publications like Science News *benefit from their research because major peer-reviewed journals often will not print papers on questionable studies, as indicated in the article.*

In this case, University of Amsterdam researchers found that, in theory, a machine might be able to run forever fueled on kinetic energy produced by random temperature changes among gas molecules. If the theory holds true, and no waste heat is produced and no additional energy is required to jump-start the random heat fluctuations, then the described system might break the second law of thermodynamics. It is sort of a catch-22 right now. If a researcher believes he or she has broken the law, the study often does not receive much attention in the scientific community. Nevertheless, if someone does truly break the law, we would not waste energy, and technology forever would be changed in miraculous ways that would change all of our lives for the better. —JV

"Breaking the Law: Can Quantum Mechanics + Thermodynamics = Perpetual Motion?"
by Peter Weiss
Science News, October 7, 2000

Hopeful inventors have for centuries tried to create machines that would run forever: gizmos such as wheels that turn unceasingly with no motor to drive them and engines that endlessly exploit the heat in the oceans to power ships.

The consequences of devising such perpetual motion machines would be wondrous because these tools would unleash energy without consuming fuel.

Despite the machines' appeal, no one has ever succeeded in making one. Physicists attribute that

miserable track record to the fact that the devices would defy fundamental laws of thermodynamics. Given that scientific lawlessness, most researchers don't give perpetual motion half a thought.

Recently, however, several groups of scientists have taken a fresh look at the concept. They propose that the peculiarities of quantum mechanics permit what seem to be violations of one of the fundamental laws—at least on a microscopic scale.

Quantum theory, which stands out already for its bizarre consequences, describes the behavior of extremely small objects such as atoms and other elementary particles. If verified, the new findings in the realm of quantum thermodynamics might indicate that a certain class of perpetual motion machines is, in fact, possible.

Not surprisingly, these new proposals are getting a chilly reception from many physicists, even though one of the three recent theoretical reports appeared in the highly regarded journal *Physical Review Letters* (*PRL*). Skeptics note, for example, that the innovative arguments in favor of perpetual motion have yet to be put to the test in working devices. They also say that the theory behind the claim may have subtle, but fatal, flaws.

Two Categories

Scientists divide perpetual motion schemes into two categories depending on whether they violate the first or second law of thermodynamics.

The first law says that energy can't be created or destroyed.

The second law clamps a strong constraint on physical devices that do useful work by tapping the energy of something hot, like steam or burning fuel. The law requires that some energy must flow from one heat source to something else at a lower temperature. For example, a car engine must cough its exhaust heat into a cooler environment, not a hotter one. The take-home message of the second law is that not all of the heat source's energy can go into doing work. Some must be wasted.

Perpetual motion schemes that rely on violations of the first law continue to be booed off stage by the scientific establishment. "This is something we don't dare to do," says theorist Theo M. Nieuwenhuizen of the University of Amsterdam.

Nevertheless, he adds, when he and a colleague probed the second law, they uncovered a route to feasible perpetual motion. Nieuwenhuizen and Armen E. Allahverdyan of CEA/Saclay in Gif-sur-Yvette, France, which is outside Paris, describe their work in the Aug. 28 *PRL*.

Testing the boundaries of the second law has been a sport for many physics luminaries including the late Richard P. Feynman. Each claim of a phenomenon that violates that law has stirred animated debate, and none has held up to scrutiny.

James Clerk Maxwell, the 19th-century scientific giant who came up with the theory of electromagnetism, offered a famous second-law challenge in 1867. He imagined a tiny being, a "demon," who could observe and manipulate individual molecules and, by doing so, overthrow the second law.

Here's how: The imp could sit inside a gas-filled box that was divided by a partition with a small door in it. Because of random thermal fluctuations, some molecules in the gas would have more kinetic energy than others. The demon would open the door only to let the fastest molecules—those with the greatest kinetic energy—pass to the other side. That would transform what began as a uniform-temperature box into two sections at different temperatures—the second law's prerequisite for accomplishing useful work, Maxwell reasoned.

Likewise, in their *PRL* report, Allahverdyan and Nieuwenhuizen come to what they themselves assess as an "appalling" conclusion: Useful work might emerge from a single heat reservoir as if one of Maxwell's demons were at work. Although the researchers consider only an abstract mathematical model, they say their equations might apply to certain real-world systems of particles, albeit ones at a temperature close to absolute zero.

In each of their perpetual motion scenarios, a minuscule "test particle" interacts with a surrounding bath of other particles. Think of a dust speck in a droplet of water. Viewed under a microscope, the speck jiggles incessantly as it is constantly bombarded by water molecules—a phenomenon called Brownian motion. Allahverdyan and Nieuwenhuizen have analyzed a similar phenomenon that occurs on a much smaller scale.

Examples of their scenarios include an atom entering an extremely cold metal box filled with bouncing microwave photons or an electron injected into a frigid crystal filled with phonons, the vibrations of lattice atoms.

The researchers propose retrieving energy from those systems by pumping them with a smaller amount of energy. In the microwave case, they envision penetrating the box with a magnetic field having a strength that varies in a cyclical manner. For the crystal, a periodic variation in applied pressure could do the trick, Allahverdyan says.

If the particles in the system vibrate in a particular way, the energy can be recaptured, the researchers contend. The pattern needed to make this happen, known as an anharmonic vibration, requires that the speed of the vibrations depend on their size. The mathematical model indicates that the pumping would release more energy from the system than it would drive into it. And that opens the door to the coveted perpetual motion.

Foiled Attempt

Various analysts have found that Maxwell's demon would require energy to carry out his task, thereby foiling his attempt to circumvent the second law. "You have to feed the demon," Nieuwenhuizen explains. Even a demon who scarcely moves a muscle to carry out his task would still need information about the molecules he sorts—and information is a form of energy, physicists have concluded.

Nieuwenhuizen and Allahverdyan, however, say that they've come across theoretical evidence for quantum systems that wouldn't require the influx of energy that a demon would need. "Quantum mechanics is doing what the demon is supposed to do," Nieuwenhuizen says, but quantum mechanics doesn't need to be fed.

Here's why. Classical physics portrays fundamental particles, such as atoms and electrons, as tiny billiard balls. Quantum mechanics, on the other hand, also represents them as waves. According to that wave nature, elementary particles extend across space and interact with each other through the overlapping of their crests and troughs.

The extended interaction, known as quantum coherence, gives quantum systems their remarkable character. It permits electrons to flow without resistance through superconductors and superfluid helium to mysteriously climb out of a cup of its own accord.

In the systems that they consider, Allahverdyan and Nieuwenhuizen stipulate that the extended interactions between particles be strong enough that another even stranger type of interaction, known as entanglement, also takes place. Entangled particles share a single quantum state, so that whatever happens to one immediately affects the other, even if they are widely separated.

A jolt of energy injected into a classical heat bath— as would happen by, say, dropping hot coals into a swimming pool—quickly peters out into random motions of molecules, slightly raising the bath's temperature. As the so-far universal failure of Maxwell's demon shows, once the energy has dissipated, the process can't be reversed.

In the systems studied by Allahverdyan and Nieuwenhuizen, however, quantum coherence and entanglement keep the energy accessible. It roams incessantly among the particles and waves. For example, when an atom enters a microwave cavity—or an electron penetrates a lattice—it joins in a back-and-forth exchange of energy and momentum.

With all that quantum-scale activity going on, the researchers asked whether thermodynamics theory—including its second law—could be applied to these systems. One prerequisite for using thermodynamics theory is that the system should settle down to a balanced, unchanging state, an equilibrium, at a slightly higher temperature. But, that's not happening in their model.

So, they conclude that thermodynamics doesn't apply. They argue that their theoretical system doesn't actually violate the second law; the violation is only "apparent." Yet they hold that their system still achieves what has long been considered impossible—it wangles useful work out of a single heat reservoir.

"The point with perpetual motion is whether you can work with one reservoir," Nieuwenhuizen remarks. "Here, we have a case where that is possible."

Quantum Route

Two other scientific reports in the past year also argue for a quantum route to perpetual motion. In one, Alexey V. Nikulov of the Russian Academy of Sciences' Institute of Microelectronics Technology and High Purity Materials in Chernogolovka, which is near Moscow, focuses on a hollow ring of deeply chilled superconducting material with electrons circulating in its walls. By switching superconductivity on and off in a segment of the ring, Nikulov argues, random thermal fluctuations would generate a useful voltage thereby violating the second law.

In the other report, theorists Vladislav Cápek and Jiri Bok, both of Charles University in Prague, the Czech Republic, propose that violations might take place even in room-temperature interactions, say, between ions and biomolecules. Indeed, Cápek told *Science News*, those breakdowns of the second law might already be occurring in living systems.

There's a caveat that applies to all three reports. None actually claims to make truly perpetual motion possible. If the first law could be violated, a machine could operate forever. However, a perpetual motion machine of the second type—a second-law violator—is powered by the kinetic energy of the reservoir. So, the machine's motion would stop when the bath's temperature hits absolute zero, just as an engine running out of gas would stop. This means that the motion of such a machine wouldn't be perpetual after all.

Neither the Russian nor Czech work was published [in] prominent venues such as *PRL*. The work of Cápek and Bok appeared in the December 1999 *Czech Journal of Physics*. Nikulov's study hasn't been published; it's posted to the physics preprint server on the Internet (http://xxx.lanl.gov/abs/physics/9912022).

How does a perpetual motion claim get into the austere, international, and highly respected *Physical Review Letters*? According to Gene Wells, one of the journal's editors, the quantum world remains so puzzling that the editor of the Allahverdyan-Nieuwenhuizen submission didn't balk. "As long as [the proposed second-law violation] is in that quantum regime, I'm not that troubled," Wells says.

After all, even the sacred first law's conservation of energy breaks down in the quantum realm, albeit in a limited way, he notes. That's because Heisenberg's uncertainty principle allows energy momentarily to appear from nothing, although it must be quickly paid back.

However, any perpetual motion schemes based on classical physics would trouble Wells. "If [the analysis] were purely classical, we, of course, would suspect it and may not even send it out to be reviewed," he says.

Not Buying It

Although stating their case in *PRL* gives Allahverdyan and Nieuwenhuizen clout, many thermodynamics specialists still aren't buying their arguments. "Such breakthroughs have happened in science before," confesses Bjarne Andresen of the University of Copenhagen, "but I do not believe that this is another one."

Quantum information theorist Barbara M. Terhal of IBM T. J. Watson Research Center in Yorktown Heights, N.Y., notes that Allahverdyan and Nieuwenhuizen are working with a mathematical entity, not actual physical systems. "If they did a more careful analysis based on the physics," she ventures, "they would see nothing going on."

Physical chemist John Ross of Stanford University isn't ready to draw any conclusions, but he's not expecting much. "It's easy to say foolish things about thermodynamics, and some very wise people have said foolish things," he cautions.

Others, however, feel that the new research may be on a promising path. "The violation of the second law at very low temperatures for certain systems is real," says Mikhail Anisimov of the University of Maryland in College Park.

William G. Unruh of the University of British Columbia in Vancouver explains that a decade ago, he and other physicists came upon the same quantum phenomenon that Allahverdyan and Nieuwenhuizen are probing, but the earlier workers didn't claim the possibility of perpetual motion. However, the new research goes further than the early work by, for instance, examining anharmonic vibration, Unruh points out.

Nonetheless, he comments, "my strong suspicion is that the amount of energy you have to stick in . . . is as much energy as you get out."

Igor M. Sokolov of the University of Freiburg in Germany thinks the *PRL* authors are onto something, though not necessarily a breakdown of the second law. They may have discovered unnoticed flaws in the mathematical tools used to describe quantum systems, he says.

On the other hand, if they're right about perpetual motion, "it could give rise to a couple of Nobel prizes," he muses.

Dramatic Impact

If verified, any second-law violations would almost certainly have a dramatic impact on the scientific world. However, the practical consequences of these reports could still prove minuscule.

Nikulov has already calculated the power that each of his proposed superconductive rings would generate. The device "cannot solve the energy problem. Its power is very weak," he concludes. Nonetheless, systems made up of many rings would generate enough energy to serve as direct-current sources in low-power circuits or to run microscopic refrigeration systems, he argues.

Nieuwenhuizen says that he's given little thought to harnessing the unusual proposed energy source or how much energy it might provide. Perhaps the technique would provide a way to cool also-hypothetical quantum computers, Allahverdyan suggests.

None of these possible applications seem like much by the standards of 19th-century dreamers and their hopes of sea-water-powered, transoceanic voyages. In the thermal fluctuations of a heat bath that's already nearly at absolute zero, there's too little energy for those visions. There's only enough, Nieuwenhuizen concedes, so that "a little quantum boat could cross a little quantum ocean."

2 Thermodynamics, Fossil Fuels, and Power Supply

Some form of petroleum probably fuels one or more machines that you rely upon daily. Cars, as they are designed today, need gasoline. Computers need electricity, which is created at power plants that often require coal-fueled generators. Stoves and central heating systems use either natural gas or electricity, both of which usually require—you guessed it—a petroleum fuel. It is no wonder that the petroleum industry has been such a lucrative one over recent centuries.

Most of us, therefore, encounter petroleum either directly or indirectly on a regular basis, and yet even the experts have poorly understood this substance. This paper provides a very thorough overview as to how petroleum forms beneath Earth's surface. Pressure and temperature conditions must be just right for the process to occur. Among the interesting new findings here is that petroleum can form only at certain depths, which are much deeper than previously stated measurements. As you will read, the *second law of thermodynamics regulates fossil fuel's formation.*

Petroleum, as the paper states, is a hydrogen-carbon system. Get rid of the carbon, and you get rid of a lot of the fuel's harmful pollutants. That is exactly what researchers are now trying to do by studying how hydrogen can be used by itself, without the chemical bond with carbon. —JV

"The Evolution of Multicomponent Systems at High Pressures: VI. The Thermodynamic Stability of the Hydrogen–Carbon System: The Genesis of Hydrocarbons and the Origin of Petroleum"
by J. F. Kenney, Vladimir A. Kutcherov, Nikolai A. Bendeliani, and Vladimir A. Alekseev
Proceedings of the National Academy of Sciences, August 20, 2002

The spontaneous genesis of hydrocarbons that comprise natural petroleum have been analyzed by chemical thermodynamic-stability theory. The constraints imposed on chemical evolution by the second law of thermodynamics are briefly reviewed, and the effective prohibition of transformation, in the regime of temperatures and pressures characteristic of the near-surface crust of the Earth, of biological molecules into hydrocarbon molecules heavier than methane is recognized. For the theoretical analysis of this phenomenon, a general, first-principles equation of state has been developed by extending scaled particle theory and by using the technique of the factored partition function of the simplified perturbed hard-chain theory. The chemical potentials and the respective thermodynamic Affinity have been calculated for typical components of the H–C system over a range of pressures between 1 and 100 kbar (1 kbar $= 100$ MPa) and at temperatures consistent with those of the depths of the Earth at such pressures. The theoretical analyses establish that the normal alkanes, the homologous hydrocarbon group of lowest chemical potential, evolve only at pressures greater than ≈ 30 kbar, excepting only the lightest, methane. The pressure of 30 kbar corresponds to depths of ≈ 100 km. For experimental verification of the predictions of the theoretical analysis, a special high-pressure apparatus has been designed that permits investigations at pressures to 50 kbar and temperatures to 1,500°C and also allows rapid cooling while maintaining high pressures. The high-pressure genesis of petroleum hydrocarbons has been demonstrated using only the reagents solid iron oxide, FeO, and marble, $CaCO_3$, 99.9 % pure and wet with triple-distilled water.

Natural petroleum is a hydrogen–carbon (H–C) system, in distinctly nonequilibrium states, composed of mixtures of highly reduced hydrocarbon molecules, all of very high chemical potential and most in the liquid phase. As such, the phenomenon of the terrestrial existence of natural petroleum in the near-surface crust of the Earth has presented several challenges, most of which have remained unresolved until recently. The primary scientific problem of petroleum has been the existence and genesis of the individual hydrocarbon molecules themselves: how, and under what thermodynamic conditions, can such highly reduced molecules of high chemical potential evolve?

The scientific problem of the genesis of hydrocarbons of natural petroleum, and consequentially of the origin of natural petroleum deposits, regrettably has been one too much neglected by competent physicists and chemists; the subject has been obscured by diverse, unscientific hypotheses, typically connected with the rococo hypothesis (1) that highly reduced hydrocarbon molecules of high chemical potentials might somehow evolve from highly oxidized biotic molecules of low chemical potential. The scientific problem of the spontaneous evolution of the hydrocarbon molecules comprising natural petroleum is one of chemical thermodynamic-stability theory. This problem does *not* involve the properties of rocks where petroleum might be found or of microorganisms observed in crude oil.

This paper is organized into five parts. The first section reviews briefly the formalism of modern thermodynamic-stability theory, the theoretical framework for the analysis of the genesis of hydrocarbons and the H–C system, as similarly for any system.

The second section examines, applying the constraints of thermodynamics, the notion that hydrocarbons might evolve spontaneously from biological molecules. Here are described the spectra of chemical potentials of hydrocarbon molecules, particularly the naturally occurring ones present in petroleum. Interpretation of the significance of the relative differences between the chemical potentials of the hydrocarbon system and those of biological molecules, applying the dictates of thermodynamic-stability theory, disposes of any hypothesis of an origin for hydrocarbon molecules from biological matter, excepting only the lightest, methane.

In the third section is described a first-principles, statistical mechanical formalism, developed from an extended representation of scaled particle theory (SPT) appropriate for mixtures of aspherical hard-body molecules combined with a mean-field representation of the long-range, attractive component of the inter-molecular potential.

In the fourth section, the thermodynamic Affinity developed using this formalism establishes that the hydrocarbon molecules peculiar to natural petroleum are high-pressure polymorphs of the H–C system, similarly as diamond and lonsdaleite are to graphite for the elemental carbon system, and evolve only in thermo-dynamic regimes of pressures greater than 25–50 kbar (1 kbar = 100 MPa).

The fifth section reports the experimental results obtained using equipment specially designed to test the predictions of the previous sections. Application of pressures to 50 kbar and temperatures to 1,500°C upon solid (and obviously abiotic) $CaCO_3$ and FeO wet with triple-distilled water, all in the absence of any initial hydrocarbon or biotic molecules, evolves the suite of petroleum fluids: methane, ethane, propane, butane, pentane, hexane, branched isomers of those compounds, and the lightest of the n-alkene series.

1. Thermodynamic Stability and the Evolution of Multicomponent Systems

Central to any analysis of chemical stability is the thermodynamic Affinity, $A(\{\mu_i\})$, which determines the direction of evolution of a system in accordance with the second law of thermodynamics as expressed by De Donder's inequality, $dQ' = Ad \geq 0$ (2). The Affinity of an n-component, multiphase system of p phases involving r chemical reactions is given as

$$A = \sum_{p=1}^{r} A_p = -\sum_{p=1}^{r} \sum_{a=1}^{p} \sum_{i=1}^{n} v_{i,p} \mu_i^{\alpha}(p, T, \{n_j\}) \qquad [1]$$

in which $\mu_{i,\rho}$ and $v_{i,\rho}$ are the chemical potential and stoichiometric coefficients of the ith component in the ρth reaction, respectively; α designates the respective phase.

The second law states that the internal production of entropy is always positive for every spontaneous transformation. Therefore, the thermodynamic Affinity (Eq. **1**) must always be positive, and the direction of evolution of any system must always obey the inequalities:

$$dS_{\text{int}} = \begin{cases} \dfrac{1}{T} \sum_p A_p \, d_p \xi_p = -\dfrac{1}{T} \sum_{p=1}^{r} \sum_{a=1}^{p} \sum_{i=1}^{n} v_{i,p} \mu_i^{\alpha}(p, T, \{n_j\}) d\xi_p \\ \sum_k F_k \, dX_k \end{cases} \geq 0$$

$$[2]$$

The inequalities in Eq. **2** express the irreversibility of spontaneous transitions and state that for a spontaneous evolution of a system from any state, A, to any other state, B, the free enthalpy of state B must be less than that of state A, and at no point between the two may the free enthalpy be greater than that of state A or less than that of state B.

The sum of the products on the second line of inequality in Eq. **2**, of the thermodynamic Affinities and the differential of the variables of extent, $d\xi\rho$, is always positive, and the circumstance for which the change of internal entropy is zero defines equilibrium, from which there is no spontaneous evolution. This is De Donder's inequality.

The sum of products on the second line of inequality in Eq. **2** deserves particular note. In the second line of Eq. **2**, F_k and dX_k are general thermodynamic forces and flows, respectively, and subsume Newton's rule, $\vec{F}=m\vec{a}$ as a special case (3, 4). The expression in the second line of Eq. **2** states further that for any circumstance for which the Affinity does not vanish, there exists a generalized thermodynamic force that drives the system toward equilibrium. The constraints of this expression assure that an apple, having disconnected from its bough, does not fall, say, half way to the ground and there stop (a phenomenon not prohibited by the first law) but must continue to fall until the ground. These constraints force a chemically reactive system to evolve always toward the state of lowest thermodynamic Affinity.

Thus, the evolution of a chemically reactive, multi-component system may be determined at any temperature, pressure, or composition whenever the chemical potentials of its components are known. To ascertain the thermodynamic regime of the spontaneous evolution of hydrocarbons, their chemical potentials must be determined.

No consideration has been given in the foregoing discussion of chemical thermodynamic stability to the rate of increase of the variables of extent, $d\xi\rho$. Such is the subject of chemical kinetics, not stability theory. The rate at which a reaction might occur cannot alter its direction as determined by the second law of thermodynamics; otherwise the second law would not exist. The evolution of a system can admit intermediate states, in which one (or more) intermediate product might possess a chemical potential considerably greater than that of any of the initial reagents. The presence of a selected catalyst can enhance a fast reaction, and if the system is removed rapidly from thermodynamic environment at which such reactions proceeding to the final state occur, the intermediate product(s) can be separated. The petrochemical industry routinely operates such processes. However, such complex industrial processes are not mimicked spontaneously in the natural world.

2. The Thermodynamic Energy Spectrum of the H–C System and the Effective Prohibition of Low-Pressure Genesis of Hydrocarbons

The thermodynamic energy spectrum of the chemical potentials (molar Gibbs energies of formation, ΔG_f) of the H–C system at standard temperature and pressure

[(STP, 298.15 K; 1 atm (1 atm = 101.3 kPa)] is available from tables of chemical data (5). The chemical potentials of naturally occurring members of the of the H–C system at STP are shown graphically in Fig. 1 [in the original article]. Examination of the energy spectrum of these chemical potentials of the H–C system establishes at once that, at STP, the chemical potentials of the entire hydrocarbon system are remarkable for both their characteristic *increase* with degree of polymerization as well as their linear, and almost constant, magnitude of such increase with carbon number. With increasing polymerization, the *n*-alkane molecules manifest increased chemical potential of very approximately 2.2 kcal per added carbon atom or CH_2 unit. (There exist also branched isomers, the chemical potentials of which differ from such of the normal configuration by, typically, 2–4 %.) Such increase in chemical potential with increased degree of polymerization contrasts strongly with the thermodynamic spectrum of the highly oxidized biotic carbon ("organic") compounds of the hydrogen–carbon–oxygen (H–C–O) system, which manifest consistently *decreasing* chemical potentials with increasing polymerization. This latter property allows the high degree of polymerization and complexity of the biotic compounds.

Examination of the H–C–O system of oxidized carbon compounds establishes that the chemical potentials of almost all biotic compounds lie far below that of methane, the least energetic of the reduced hydrocarbon compounds, typically by several hundred kcal/mol. Although there exist biotic molecules of unusually high chemical potential such as β-carotene ($C_{40}H_{56}$), vitamin D ($C_{38}H_{44}O$), and some of the pheromone hormones, such compounds are relatively rare by abundance. They are produced by biological systems only when the producing entity is alive (and at formidable metabolic cost to the producing entity), and the production ceases with the death of the entity. Such compounds are not decomposition products of other biotic compounds and are labile and themselves decompose rapidly. For these foregoing reasons, such compounds cannot be considered relevant to the subject of the origin of natural petroleum.

The properties of the thermodynamic energy spectrum of the H–C and H–C–O systems, together with the constraints of the second law (Eq. 2) establish three crucial properties of natural petroleum:

(i) The H–C system that constitutes natural petroleum is a metastable one in a very nonequilibrium state. At low pressures, all heavier hydrocarbon molecules are thermodynamically unstable against decomposition into methane and carbon, as similarly is diamond into graphite.

(ii) Methane does not polymerize into heavy hydrocarbon molecules at low pressures at any temperature. Contrarily, increasing temperature (at low pressures) must increase the rate of decomposition of heavier hydrocarbons into methane and carbon.

(iii) Any hydrocarbon compound generated at low pressures, heavier than methane, would be unstable and driven to the stable equilibrium state of methane and carbon.

These conclusions have been demonstrated amply by a century of refinery engineering practice. The third conclusion has been demonstrated by many unsuccessful laboratory attempts to convert biotic molecules into hydrocarbons heavier than methane.

There are three generic chemical processes that deserve specific consideration: the "charcoal burner's," "bean-eater's," and "octane-enhanced bean-eater's" reactions. All describe limited reactions by which a highly oxidized biotic molecule can react to produce elemental carbon when "carried" by a more thorough oxidation process. In both the following examples, the simple carbohydrate, sugar $C_6H_{12}O_6$, is used as a typical biotic reagent; the same reasoning and results hold also for any of the highly oxidized biotic compounds.

The charcoal burner's reaction is:

$$C_6H_{12}O_6 \ 3 \rightarrow 6C + 6H_2O. \qquad \text{[3]}$$

The chemical potential of water vapor at STP is −54.636 kcal/mol. The thermodynamic Affinity for the charcoal burner's reaction (Reaction 3) to produce amorphous carbon, or graphite, is 109.10 kcal. Therefore, the genesis of coal from biological detritus in an oxygen-poor environment is permitted by the second law. However, the thermodynamic Affinity for the charcoal burner's reaction to produce diamond is 105.02 kcal, the quantity of which is also positive, and therefore not immediately prohibited by the second law as expressed solely by de Donder's inequality, the first of equations (Eq. 2). Nonetheless, no charcoal burner ever scrabbles through his ashes hoping to find diamonds. Such reasonable behavior demonstrates an effective appreciation of the dictates of the second law as expressed by Eq. 2. In this case, the generalized force is the difference in thermodynamic Affinity between the reactions for graphite and diamond, respectively, $\delta F = \delta A/T$, which, in the regime of temperatures and pressures of the near-surface crust of the Earth, assures always the genesis of graphite, never diamond. Similarly, for reactions involving hydrocarbons heavier than methane, the same generalized force, $\delta A/T$, always drives the system toward the state of lowest free enthalpy, i.e., methane plus free carbon.

The bean-eater's reaction is:

$$C_6H_{12}O_6 \rightarrow 3CH_4 + 3CO_2. \qquad [4]$$

The chemical potentials at STP for the simple carbohydrate $C_6H_{12}O_6$, methane, and carbon dioxide are –218.720, –12.130, and –94.260 kcal/mol, respectively. The thermodynamic Affinity for the reaction accordingly is 100.42 kcal/mol and therefore permitted by the second law. Indeed, reactions of the type in Reaction 4 are typical of those by which methane is produced in swamps, sewers, and the bowels of herbivores.

The octane-enhanced bean-eater's reaction is:

$$C_6H_{12}O_6 \rightarrow 2CH_4 + 3CO_2 + \tfrac{1}{8}C_8H_{18} + \tfrac{7}{8}H_2. \qquad [5]$$

Since the chemical potential of n-octane is 4.290 kcal/mol at STP, and that of molecular hydrogen is zero,

the thermodynamic Affinity for the octane-enhanced bean-eater's reaction is $A = (100.42 -12.130 - 4.290/8) = 87.70$ kcal/mol, still positive and thereby not prohibited outright by the constraints of De Donder's inequality. However, no biochemical investigation has ever observed a molecule of any hydrocarbon heavier than methane resulting from the decomposition of biological detritus. After a meal of, e.g., Boston baked beans, one does experience biogenic methane, but *not* biogenic octane. No such process produces heavier hydrocarbons, for such a process would involve effectively a reaction of low-pressure methane polymerization, similarly as the effective prohibition of the evolution of diamonds by the charcoal burner's reaction. In the previous section, we described the industrial technique by which useful intermediate products can be obtained by controlling the reaction process. The Fischer–Tropsch process uses reactions essentially identical to Reaction 5 to generate liquid petroleum fuels from the combustion of coal, wood, or other biotic matter. However, the highly controlled industrial Fischer–Tropsch process does not produce, spontaneously and uncontrolled, the commonly observed large accumulations of natural petroleum.

The foregoing properties of natural petroleum and the effective prohibition by the second law of thermodynamics of its spontaneous genesis from highly oxidized biological molecules of low chemical potentials were clearly understood in the second half of the 19th century by chemists and thermodynamicists such as Berthelot and later confirmed by others including Sokolov, Biasson, and Mendeleev. However, the problem of how and in what regime of temperature and pressure hydrogen and carbon combine to form the particular H–C system manifested by natural petroleum remained. The resolution of this problem had to wait a century for the development of modern atomic and molecular theory, quantum statistical mechanics, and many-body theory. This problem now has been resolved theoretically by determination of the chemical potentials and the thermodynamic Affinity of the H–C system using modern quantum statistical mechanics and has also now been demonstrated experimentally with specially designed high-pressure apparatus.

3. Calculation of the Thermodynamic Affinity Using SPT and the Formalism of the Simplified Perturbed Hard-Chain Theory (SPHCT)

To calculate the thermodynamic Affinity of a distribution of compounds of the H–C system in general regimes of temperature and pressure, one must use a rigorous mathematical formalism developed from first-principles statistical mechanical argument. No approximate, or interpolated, formalism developed for the low-pressure regime can suffice. A sufficiently rigorous formalism has been developed by extending the SPT equation of state of Pavlícek, Nezbeda, and Boublík (6, 7), for mixtures of convex hard-body systems, combined with the formalism of the SPHCT (8).

Following the procedure enunciated originally by Bogolyubov (9) and developed further by Feynmann (10) and Yukhnovski (11), a factored partition function

is used that employs a reference system: $Q = Q^{\text{ref}}Q^{\text{vdW}}$. The reference system used is that of the hard-body fluid as described rigorously by SPT (12–15). The description of the hard-body fluid by SPT is one of the *few exactly solvable* problems in statistical mechanics. This property is especially valuable because the thermodynamic evolution of a system at high pressures is determined almost entirely by the variable components that are obtained from the reference system.

For mixtures of hard-body particles of different sizes and shapes, SPT generates the following analytical expression for the contribution to the pressure of the hard-core reference system:

$$p^{\text{ref}} = k_B T\rho \left[1 + \left(\frac{\eta}{(1-\eta)} + \frac{rs}{\rho(1-\eta)^2} + \frac{qs^2(1-2n) + 5rs\eta^2}{3\rho^3(1-\eta)^3} \right) \right]$$

$$= (\rho^{\text{IG}} + \rho^{\text{hc}}), \qquad\qquad [6]$$

in which the geometric compositional variables, r, s, and η, are defined by the Steiner–Kihara equations:

$$r = \rho \sum_i x_i \tilde{R}_i, \quad q = \rho \sum_i x_i \tilde{R}_i^2, \quad s = \rho \sum_i x_i \tilde{S}_i,$$

$$\left. v = \sum_i x_i \tilde{V}_i \quad \eta = \rho \sum_i x_i \tilde{V}_i = \rho v \right\} . \qquad [7]$$

(A thorough discussion of the Steiner–Kihara parameters may be found in ref. 16.) The following geometric functions are introduced: $\alpha = rs/3v$, and $\gamma = \langle r^2 \rangle / \langle r \rangle^2$. The geometric parameter α is the multicomponent analogue of the Boublík parameter of asphericity for a single-component fluid, $\alpha^{\mathrm{B}} = \tilde{R}\tilde{S}/(3\tilde{V})$, and may be interpreted as the system's weighted degree of asphericity. The parameter γ has no analogue in a single-component fluid, for which it is always equal to unity. γ might be interpreted as a parameter of interference that measures the degree of difference in the mean component dimensions of radii. When these definitions are used, the Boublík equation (Eq. **6**) can be written in a simple form as

$$p^{\mathrm{ref}} = k_{\mathrm{B}}T\rho\left[1 + \frac{c_1\eta + c_2\eta^2 + c_3\eta^3}{(1-\eta)^3}\right], \qquad [8]$$

in which c_1, c_2, and c_3 are variables of composition that depend on the combined geometries of the molecular components and their fractional abundances: $c_1 = 3\alpha + 1$, $c_2 = 3\alpha(\alpha\gamma - 1) - 2$, and $c_3 = 1 - \alpha(6\alpha\gamma - 5)$.

Similarly, the contribution of the reference system to the free enthalpy may be written, as

$$G^{\mathrm{ref}} = Nk_{\mathrm{B}}T\left[\sum_i x_i\ln\left(\frac{(n_i\lambda_i^3)}{V}\right) + \eta\left(\frac{I + J\eta + K\eta^2}{(1-\eta)^3}\right) - c_3\ln(1-\eta)\right], \qquad [9]$$

in which $I = 2c_1 - c_3$, $J = -1/2(3c_1 - 3c_2 - 5c_3)$, and $K = 1/6(3c_1 - 3c_2 - 3c_3)$. When these identities are used, the contribution of the reference system to the pressure and the free enthalpy become simplified functions of the packing-fraction, η, and the geometric compositional variables, α and γ.

The contributions to the pressure and the chemical potentials from the long-range van der Waals component of the intermolecular potential are described using the formalism of the SPHCT (17–19). The SPHCT uses the mean-field technique (20) of the Bethe–Peierls–Prigogine "lattice-gas" model, in which has been applied the shape-independent scattering formalism (21). As demonstrated previously (22) at elevated pressures, the pressure and chemical potential are dominated by their respective hard-core components, and the attractive component is several orders of magnitude smaller and of little consequence. The representation of the attractive components of the pressure and chemical potential used has been that developed for the SPHCT by Sandler (23), Donohue and Prausnitz (19), and Lee and Chao (24) using the mixing rules of Kim $et\ al.$ (25). The Prigogine shape c factors used by the SPHCT are related to the Boublík geometric parameters such that $c_i = (1 + 3\tilde{R}_i\tilde{S}_i/\tilde{V}_i\ )$ and $V_i^* = \tilde{V}_i\ (1 + \alpha_i)$. The values of V_i and α_i were taken from van Pelt $et\ al.$ (26). The chemical potential of the i-th specie of a multicomponent system is given by $\mu_i = \mu_i^- + \mu_i^{ref} + \mu_i^{vdW}$, in which μ_i^- represents the reference value of the chemical potential at STP.

4. The Evolution of the Normal Alkanes, Ethane, Hexane, and Decane from Methane at High Pressures

At STP, methane possesses the lowest chemical potential and is the only thermodynamically stable hydrocarbon. At low pressures and all temperatures, all hydrocarbons are thermodynamically unstable relative to methane or methane plus carbon (either graphite or amorphous carbon). At normal temperatures and pressures, the evolution of methane will dominate and effectively exhaust the H–C system of its elemental components. Because methane is the sole hydrocarbon specie that is thermodynamically stable at low pressures, the chemical Affinities of each of the heavier species have been calculated in comparison with methane. Accordingly, the chemical Affinity calculated for the thermodynamic stability of, for example, the methane ↔ (n-octane + hydrogen) system is that for the reaction $CH_4 \rightarrow 1/8 \ C_8H_{18} + 7/8 \ H_2$.

The chemical potentials of the hydrocarbon and methane molecules and the resulting thermodynamic Affinities of the (methane → hydrocarbon + hydrogen) system have been evaluated for the n-alkanes from methane through $C_{20}H_{42}$. In Fig. 2 [in the original article] are shown the Gibbs energies for the set of hydrocarbons methane (CH_4) and the n-alkanes, ethane (n-C_2H_6), hexane (n-C_6H_{14}), and decane (n-$C_{10}H_{22}$). These thermodynamic variables have been determined at pressures ranging from 1 to 100,000 bar and at the supercritical temperature 1,000 K, the temperature of which corresponds conservatively to the geological regime characterized by the respective pressures of transition.

The values of the SPHCT parameters, c, η, and Y, for the individual compounds that have been used were taken from van Pelt $et\ al.$ (27), and the reference values of the chemical potentials of the pure component were taken from standard reference tables (3).

The results of the analysis are shown graphically for the temperature 1,000 K in Fig. 2 [in the original article]. These results demonstrate clearly that all hydrocarbon molecules are unstable chemically and thermodynamically relative to methane at pressures less than ≈25 kbar for the lightest, ethane, and 40 kbar for the heaviest n-alkane shown, decane.

The results of this analysis, shown graphically in Fig. 2 [in the original article], establish clearly the following:

(i) With the exception of methane, heavier hydrocarbon molecules of higher chemical potentials are not generated spontaneously in the low-pressure regime of methane synthesis.

(ii) All hydrocarbon molecules other than methane are high-pressure polymorphs of the H–C system and evolve spontaneously only at high pressures, greater than at least 25 kbar even under the most favorable circumstances.

(iii) Contrary to experience of refinery operations conducted at low pressures, heavier alkanes are *not* unstable and do *not* necessarily decompose at elevated temperatures. Contrarily, at high pressures, methane transforms into the heavier alkanes, and the transformation processes are enhanced by elevated temperatures.

The theoretical analyses reported here describe the high-pressure evolution of hydrocarbons under the *most favorable* chemical conditions. Therefore, although this analysis describes the thermodynamic stability of the H–C system, it does not explicitly do the same for the genesis of natural petroleum in the conditions of the depths of the Earth. The chemical conditions of the Earth, particularly near its surface, are oxidizing, *not* reducing; of the gases in the Earth's atmosphere and crust, hydrogen is significantly absent, and methane is a very minor constituent.

Although both methane and heavier hydrocarbons were present in the carbonaceous meteorites that participated in the accretion process of the formation of the Earth, such molecules were unlikely to have survived in their initial composition. The heat of impact that accompanied accretion most likely would have caused decomposition of heavier hydrocarbons and the release of methane. For both the theoretical analyses described in this section and the experimental investigations described in section 5, the conservative perspective has been taken that hydrocarbons evolve from the solid, abiotic carbon compounds and vestigial water present in the upper mantle of the Earth.

5. Experimental Demonstration of Hydrocarbon Genesis Under Thermodynamic Conditions Typical of the Depths of the Earth

Because the H–C system typical of petroleum is generated at high pressures and exists only as a metastable mélange at laboratory pressures, special high-pressure apparatus has been designed that permits investigations at pressures to 50 kbar and temperatures to 1,500°C, and which also allows rapid cooling while maintaining high pressures (28). The importance of this latter ability

cannot be overstated; for to examine the spontaneous reaction products, the system must be quenched rapidly to "freeze in" their high-pressure, high-temperature distribution. Such a mechanism is analogous to that which occurs during eruptive transport processes responsible for kimberlite ejecta and for the stability and occurrence of diamonds in the crust of the Earth.

Experiments to demonstrate the high-pressure genesis of petroleum hydrocarbons have been carried out using *only* 99.9 % pure solid iron oxide, FeO, and marble, $CaCO_3$, wet with triple-distilled water. There were *no* biotic compounds or hydrocarbons admitted to the reaction chamber. The use of marble instead of elemental carbon was intentionally conservative. The initial carbon compound, $CaCO_3$, is more oxidized and of lower chemical potential, all of which rendered the system more resistant to the reduction of carbon to form heavy alkanes than it would be under conditions of the mantle of the Earth. Although there has been observed igneous $CaCO_3$ (carbonatite) of mantle origin, carbon should be more reasonably expected to exist in the mantle of the Earth as an element in its dense phases: cubic (diamond), hexagonal (lonsdaleite), or random-close pack (chaoite).

Pressure in the reaction cell, as described in ref. 25, of volume 0.6 cm³ was measured by a pressure gauge calibrated using data of the phase transitions of Bi, Tl, and PbTe. The cell was heated by a cylindrical graphite heater; its temperature was measured using a chromel-alumel thermocouple and was regulated within the range $\pm 5°C$. Both stainless steel and platinum reaction cells were used; all were constructed to prevent contamination by air and provide impermeability during and after each experimental run.

The reaction cell was brought from 1 bar to 50 kbar gradually at a rate of 2 kbar/min and from room temperature to the elevated temperatures of investigation at the rate of 100 K/min. The cell and reaction chamber were held for at least 1 h at each temperature for which measurements were taken to allow the H–C system to come to thermodynamic equilibrium. The samples thereafter were quenched rapidly at the rate of 700°C/sec to 50°C and from 50°C to room temperature over several minutes while maintaining the high pressure of investigation. The pressure was then reduced gradually to 1 bar at the rate of 1 kbar/min. The reaction cell was then heated gently to desorb the hydrocarbons for mass spectrometer analysis using an HI-120 1B mass spectrometer equipped with an automatic system of computerized spectrum registration. A specially designed high-temperature gas probe allowed sampling the cell while maintaining its internal pressure.

At pressures below 10 kbar, no hydrocarbons heavier than methane were present. Hydrocarbon molecules began to evolve above 30 kbar. At 50 kbar and at the temperature of 1,500°C, the system spontaneously evolved methane, ethane, n-propane, 2-methylpropane, 2,2-dimethylpropane, n-butane, 2-methylbutane, n-pentane, 2-methylpentane, n-hexane, and n-alkanes through $C_{10}H_{22}$, ethene, n-propene, n-butene, and n-pentene in distributions characteristic of natural petroleum. The cumulative abundances of the subset of evolved hydrocarbons consisting of methane and *n*-alkanes through $n\text{-}C_6H_{14}$ are shown in Fig. 3 [in the original article] as functions of temperature. Methane (on the right scale) is present and of abundance ≈ 1 order of magnitude greater than any single component of the heavier *n*-alkanes, although as a minor component of the total H–C system. That the extent of hydrocarbon evolution becomes relatively stable as a function of temperature above $\approx 900°C$, both for the absolute abundance of the individual hydrocarbon species as well as for their relative abundances, argues that the distributions observed represent thermodynamic equilibrium for the H–C system. That the evolved hydrocarbons remain stable over a range of temperatures increasing by more than 300 K demonstrates the third prediction of the theoretical analysis: Hydrocarbon molecules heavier than methane do not decompose with increasing temperature in the high-pressure regime of their genesis.

6. Discussion and Conclusions

The pressure of 30 kbar, at which the theoretical analyses of section 4 predicts that the H–C system must evolve ethane and heavier hydrocarbon compounds, corresponds to a depth of more than 100 km. The results of the theoretical analysis shown in Fig. 2 [in the original article] clearly establish that the evolution of the molecular components of natural petroleum occur at depth *at least* as great as those of the mantle of the Earth, as shown graphically in Fig. 4 [in the original article], in which are represented the thermal and pressure lapse rates in the depths of the Earth.

As noted, the theoretical analyses reported in section 4 describe the high-pressure evolution of hydrocarbons under the *most favorable* chemical conditions. The theoretical calculations for the evolution of hydrocarbons posited the presence of methane, the genesis of which must itself be demonstrated in the depths of the Earth consistent with the pressures required for the evolution of heavier hydrocarbons. Furthermore, the multicomponent system analyzed theoretically included no oxidizing reagents that would compete with hydrogen for both the carbon and any free hydrogen. The theoretical analysis assumed also the possibility of at least a metastable presence of hydrogen. Therefore, the theoretical results must be considered as the determination of *minimum* boundary conditions for the genesis of hydrocarbons. In short, the genesis of natural petroleum must occur at depths *not less than* ≈ 100 km, well into the mantle of the Earth. The experimental observations reported in section 5 confirm theoretical predictions of section 4, and demonstrate how, under high pressures, hydrogen combines with available carbon to produce heavy hydrocarbon compounds in the geochemical environment of the depths of the Earth.

Notwithstanding the generality and first-principles rigor with which the present theoretical analysis has used, the results of the theoretical analyses here reported are robustly independent of the details of any reasonable mathematical model. The results of this theoretical analysis are strongly consistent with those developed previously by Chekaliuk and Kenney (29–32) using less accurate formal tools. The analysis of the H–C system at high pressures and temperatures has been impeded previously by the absence of reliable equations of state that could describe a chemically reactive, multicomponent system at densities higher than such of its normal liquid state in ordinary laboratory conditions and at high temperatures. The first analyses used the (plainly inadequate) Tait equation (33); later was used the quantum mechanical Law of Corresponding States (34); more recently has been applied the single-fluid model of the SPHCT (31, 32). Nonetheless, *all* analyses of the chemical stability of the H–C system have shown results that are qualitatively identical and quantitatively very similar: all show that hydrocarbons heavier than methane cannot evolve spontaneously at pressures below 20–30 kbar.

The H–C system does not spontaneously evolve heavy hydrocarbons at pressures less than ≈30 kbar, even in the most favorable thermodynamic environment. The H–C system evolves hydrocarbons under pressures found in the mantle of the Earth and at temperatures consistent with that environment.

1. Lomonosov, M. V. (1757) *Slovo o Reshdinii Metallov ot Tryaseniya Zemli* (Akadimii Nauk, St. Petersburg).

2. De Donder, T. (1936) *L'Affinité* (Gautier-Villars, Paris).

3. Kondepudi, D. & Prigogine, I. (1998) *Modern Thermodynamics: From Heat Engines to Dissipative Structures* (Wiley, New York).

4. Prigogine, I. & Defay, R. (1954) *Chemical Thermodynamics* (Longmans, London).

5. U.S. Bureau of Standards (1946–1952) *Selected Properties of Hydrocarbons*, A.P.I. Project 41 (U.S. Bureau of Standards, Washington, DC).

6. Pavlícek, J., Nezbeda, I. & Boublík, T. (1979) *Czech. J. Phys.* B29, 1061–1070.

7. Boublík, T. (1981) *Mol. Phys.* 42, 209–216.

8. Prigogine, I. (1957) *Molecular Theory of Solutions* (North–Holland, Amsterdam).

9. Bogolyubov, N. N. (1946) *Problems of a Dynamical Theory in Statistical Mechanics* (GITTL, Moscow).

10. Feynman, R. P. (1972) *Statistical Mechanics: A Set of Lectures* (Addison–Wesley, New York).

11. Yukhnovskii, I. R. (1987) *Phase Transitions of the Second Order: The Method of Collective Variables* (World Scientific, Singapore).

12. Reiss, H., Frisch, H. L. & Lebowitz, J. L. (1959) *J. Chem. Phys.* 31, 369–380.

13. Reiss, H., Frisch, H. L. & Lebowitz, J. L. (1964) in *The Equilibrium Theory of Classical Fluids*, eds. Frisch, H. L. & Lebowitz, J. L. (W. A. Benjamin, New York), pp. II-299–II-302.

14. Reiss, H. (1965) in *Advances in Chemical Physics*, ed. Prigogine, I. (Interscience, New York), Vol. 9, pp. 1–84.

15. Reiss, H. (1977) in *Statistical Mechanics and Statistical Methods in Theory and Application: A Tribute to Elliott W. Montroll*, ed. Landman, U. (Plenum, London), pp. 99–140.

16. Kenney, J. F. & Deiters, U. K. (2000) *Phys. Chem. Chem. Phys.* 2, 3163–3174.

17. Vera, J. H. & Prausnitz, J. M. (1972) *Chem. Eng. J.* 3, 113.

18. Beret, S. & Prausnitz, J. M. (1975) *AIChE J.* 21, 1123–1132.

19. Donohue, M. D. & Prausnitz, J. M. (1978) *AIChE J.* 24, 849–860.

20. Bethe, H. A. & Kirkwood, J. G. (1939) *J. Chem. Phys.* 7, 578–582.

21. Huang, K. & Yang, C. N. (1957) *Phys. Rev.* 105, 767–775.

22. Kenney, J. F. (1998) *Fluid Phase Equilibria* 148, 21–47.

23. Sandler, S. I. (1985) *Fluid Phase Equilibria* 19, 233–257.

24. Lee, R. J. & Chao, K. C. (1987) *Mol. Phys.* 61, 1431–1442.

25. Kim, C.-H., Vimalchand, P., Donohue, P. & Sandler, S. I. (1986) *AIChE J.* 32, 1726–1734.

26. van Pelt, A., Peters, C. J. & de Swaan Arons, J. (1991) *J. Chem. Phys.* 95, 7569–7575.

27. van Pelt, A., Peters, C. J. & de Swaan Arons, J. (1992) *Fluid Phase Equilibria* 74, 67–83.

28. Nikolaev, N. A. & Shalimov, M. D. (1999) Patent RF 1332598,MKE601; (1999) *Bull. Izobretenii (Russia)* 7, 257, 23/20.

29. Chekaliuk, E. B. (1975) in *Regularities of Formation of Commercial Oil and Gas Fields* (Naukova Dumka, Kiev, Ukraine), pp. 66–76.

30. Kenney, J. F. (1993) *Bull. A. P. S.* 38, 1508.

31. Kenney, J. F. (1995) in *Joint XV AIR/APT International Conference on High-Pressure Physics and Technology (Warsaw)*, pp. 843–845.

32. Kenney, J. F. (1997) in *The Prospects for Oil and Gas Potential of the Crystalline Basement in the Territory of Tatarstan and Volga-Kama Region*, ed. Romanov, G. V. (Russian Academy of Sciences, Kazan, Russia), pp. 43–52.

33. Chekaliuk, E. B. (1971) *The Thermodynamic Basis for the Theory of the Abiotic Genesis of Petroleum* (Naukova Dumka, Kiev, Ukraine).

34. Chekaliuk, E. B. & Kenney, J. F. (1991) *Proc. Am. Phys. Soc.* 36, 347.
35. Kudryavtsev, N. A. (1951) *Petroleum Econ.* (Neftianoye Khozyaistvo) 9, 17–29.

Reprinted with permission from *Proceedings of the National Academy of Sciences*, Vol. 99, No. 17, August 20, 2002, pp. 10976–10981. © 2002, National Academy of Sciences, U.S.A.

A popular comedy show from the early 1960s featured a hillbilly family that struck it rich thanks to a chance finding of an underground natural oil reserve. In real life, the gas and oil industry uses scientific methods to find oil reserves. As the next article explains, measuring temperatures above and below suspected hydrocarbon sources can reveal the size of the potential fuel source.

Author Lloyd Fons used an idea from the second law of thermodynamics, which states that work occurs in an irreversible process. In this case, heat created within Earth's core flows outward, where it gradually is absorbed by various elements and objects. Water again becomes an element of interest for scientists because it turns out to have more upward heat transfer ability than other, denser materials. Both hydrocarbons and water take in the heat and transfer it upward.

In theory, then, examining a possible oil reserve merely involves measuring the temperature above and below the source. The greater the difference between these two measurements, the greater the size of the reserve.

Before you get out your shovel, remember that oil is often far below the ground's surface. This article was written for oil industry experts, probably to encourage them to try out the new technique. —JV

"Temperature Anomaly Mapping Identifies Subsurface Hydrocarbons"
by Lloyd Fons
World Oil, September 2000

Utilizing the fact that buried hydrocarbons alter the upward flow of heat through earth layers offers industry another valuable exploration tool

Heat moving upward from deeper portions of the earth will arrive at various depths—and eventually to the surface—at different temperatures, depending on what type of materials (solids and fluids) it passes through. If a particular layer of subsurface material—say a hydrocarbon reservoir—has an insulating capability, the earth temperature below that layer will be higher, and temperature above it will be lower, than those below and above a noninsulating layer. Consequently, a temperature map will display a temperature anomaly above (and below) the hydrocarbon reservoir.

The following article discusses the concept of Temperature Anomaly Mapping (TAM), as it can be applied to locating subsurface hydrocarbons (insulating material), from temperature changes on the surface from one area to another. Below the surface, anomalies

in the temperature gradient may be used to tell whether additional hydrocarbons exist below a particular well's TD. The subject of TAM was introduced in a previous article;[1] and further case history applications will be presented at an October 2000 GCAGS meeting.[2]

Introduction, Theory

Although not perfect, this new hydrocarbon exploration/evaluation method may well be the most logical in the industry. It can be highly effective, and it appears to be fail-safe. The method finds hydrocarbons (quantitatively) with little reliance on other exploration data. Fundamentally, it entails construction and interpretation of temperature anomaly maps. Temperature profiles may be taken from: 1) bottomhole depths using BHT thermometers, Fig. 1 [in the original article]; 2) earth surfaces by remote sensing, Fig. 2 [in the original article]; and 3) near-surface air, and offshore water (at fixed depths below any thermocline), Fig. 3 [in the original article]. Bottomhole temperature can identify deeper prospective pay zones and indicate when to terminate drilling.

Creating five-foot-deep holes in unconsolidated sediments and measuring bottom temperature by thermocouple requires only about 20 minutes per station. To date, five-foot-depth temperature profiles have satisfactorily paralleled 100-ft-depth profiles, Fig. 4 [in original article]. This survey was completed in one day, by one person, with hand-carried equipment.

Infrared temperature surveys by either surface vehicle or airplane are limited by only the maximum speed of the survey vehicles and, occasionally, by adverse atmospheric conditions. Surveys by airplane have covered more than 600 mi, with answers obtained before breakfast.

The method will: 1) locate stratigraphic-trap reservoirs and predict reservoir shape and boundaries; 2) explore below the bottom of drilled holes; and 3) lower the cost of finding oil/gas by reducing or eliminating the need for seismic surveys and minimizing the risk of dry holes. It is simple, rapid, safe, environmentally compatible and inexpensive—permits are seldom required.

How It Works

Heat flows from within the earth to its surface, a process defined by the Second Law of Thermodynamics and Fourier's Law. Hydrocarbons tend to be more insulative to heat flow than common earth materials. Hydrocarbons, in combination with connate water are, in turn, much more insulative to upward heat flow than hydrocarbons alone.

Because of these insulating properties, hydrocarbon-rich reservoirs form relatively efficient, though imperfect, thermal barriers, resulting in a dynamic equilibrium condition of negative temperature anomalies above, and positive temperature anomalies below hydrocarbon reservoirs. The general relationship is simply stated: The greater the negative anomaly directly above a reservoir, the greater the hydrocarbon deposit below the point of measurement. The greater the positive anomaly directly below a reservoir, the greater the hydrocarbon deposit above the point of measurement. However, there is an inverse relationship between distance from hydrocarbon deposit and magnitude of observed temperature anomaly. Also, the surveying of many fields containing both oil and gas wells has found that the greatest negative anomalies have been found over the oil-productive sections of the fields.

Thermal Conductivity Misconceptions

"Thermal conductivity" is a widely misused term in our schools and in the oil and gas industry. By proper definition, it is limited to heat transfer by conduction. Contrary to common belief, the sedimentary component exhibiting the greatest upward heat transfer ability is water, not halite or quartzite. The author's experiments have shown that upward heat transfer in/of water is more than 18 times that for downward heat transfer, Fig. 5 [in the original article]. The thermal conductivity value for water is 1.39 cal/cm²-sec/°C/cm X [10^{-3}]. A common value for halite is 9.56 (range 3.11–17.2), and quartzite 10.99 (range 7.41–19.12).[3] When one multiplies the thermal conductivity value of water (1.39) by 18 (as the experiment dictates) the result is 25.02, which is greater than the value for either halite or quartzite.

There also is a convective component included in subsurface heat transfer, Fig. 6 [in the original article].

The heat transferability of porous formations cannot be accurately derived by looking up published values for thermal conductivity and multiplying those by the fraction of each component within the formation, then summing the component values. Subsurface temperature gradients increase with decreasing heat transfer ability and not necessarily with decreasing thermal conductivity. Commonly reported temperature gradients for atmosphere and ocean are almost identical (0.28°F – 0.33°F/100 ft), while the thermal conductivity of salt water is more than 30 times that of air. Near-surface, earth-gradient values (0.8°F – 1.1°F/100 ft) are more than three times those reported for air or water, while the thermal conductivity of common near-surface sediments is more than 100 times that of air.

Reservoir Property Effects

The oil in hydrocarbon reservoirs is always in contact with connate water. Oil and water are immiscible; at every oil-water interface, dissimilar molecules, with similar surface charges, are repulsed, preventing cross-gender diffusion and mixing. At each of the untold millions of immiscible boundaries, heat transfer by natural convection and/or diffusion is prevented. All other things being equal—such as temperature, fluid density, water saturation and viscosity—within commercial hydrocarbon reservoirs, the greater the porosity, the greater the insulation. This is opposite of what is observed in water zones.

One can support the concept and importance of subsurface convective heat transfer and immiscible barriers by observing that the greatest temperature gradients occur in oil producing reservoirs that are fine grained. These have the greatest number of pore spaces, highest water content per unit of porosity, and present the most immiscible oil-water boundaries per unit volumes. Porosity decreases with depth and increased geologic age, accompanied by increased matrix percentage per unit volume. Although the "thermal conductivity" of the matrix is many times that of water, sediment temperature gradients in water zones increase, rather than decrease, with depth and decreasing water content. This is just the opposite of what is stated in current literature by university and government scientists within the U.S. Scores of temperature gradients through hydrocarbon deposits as great as 100°F/100 ft have been documented.

Subsurface temperature gradient charts published in every service company log analysis handbook studied show linear subsurface temperature gradients. After plotting depth vs. temperature for more than 100,000 wells, linear gradients were not observed, Fig. 7 [in the original article]. To accept a linear gradient, one must concede that all sedimentary and igneous materials at any depth have identical thermal conductivity and/or heat transfer ability.

In developing a reliable analytical tool using earth temperature measurement, each obvious variable has been taken into account. These include time since circulation, hole size, mud density (formation pressure), time of year, mud viscosity, surface elevation and variations in lithology (percentages of sand and shale) within the intervals being studied. Even the all-too-common, unprofessional practice (by logging engineers) of estimating BHT without such notification on the log heading has been taken into account. Fortunately, none of these variables seriously handicaps the basic hydrocarbon-finding abilities of Temperature Anomaly Mapping.

Significantly, the presence or absence of faulting is of no consequence to interpretation, unless faulting is responsible for the accumulation of hydrocarbons. Under suitable common survey conditions, only the presence of hydrocarbons appears to exert major influence on the magnitude of subsurface temperatures. With diligent work, TAM technology may well lead to the finding of a considerable part of the world's remaining undiscovered hydrocarbons.

Note: The method is patented in the U.S. and Canada, and DTB Enterprises, LLC, Spring, Texas, now holds an exclusive license to use and market the system.

LITERATURE CITED

(1.) Fons, L., "Temperature method can help locate oil, gas deposits," *Oil and Gas Journal*, April 12, 1999, pp. 59–64.

(2.) Fons, L. and J. Donovan, "Temperature anomaly mapping: A risk reduction technology," to be presented at the Gulf Coast Association of Geological Societies meeting, Houston, October 2000.

(3.) Gregoriev & Meilikov, *Handbook of Physical Quantities*, CRC Press, 1997.

A challenge of your generation will be to devise and implement a way for society to move away

from fossil fuel use toward a cleaner, more sustainable form of energy. When heat energy is extracted from coal, gas, and oil, impurities are released that have been linked to numerous health problems. In addition, oil reserves are in limited supply.

While the current U.S. political administration has its eyes on mostly untapped fossil fuel sources, such as the oil found in the state of Alaska, even that supply, and others, eventually will run out. The cost to human health of using such fuels also, according to many studies, may be too high a price. For example, many reports have linked pollution from fossil fuels to climate change, which, in turn, has been linked to extinctions, to animal and plant population reductions, and even to mutations among certain species. In short, many believe that developing an alternative to fossil fuels is a necessity and not an option.

Aside from research and political limitations, one stumbling block has been how to tap the energy potential of hydrogen. A big problem with hydrogen, as you will read in this article, is that it is currently hard to store in a small space. Liquid, gas, and solid storage thus far have proven to be mostly impractical for an average-sized automobile. Quantum mechanics might provide a breakthrough, but the authors here have their doubts, at least for now. —JV

"Bottling the Hydrogen Genie"
by Frederick E. Pinkerton and Brian G. Wicke
The Industrial Physicist, February/March 2004

As the dawn of a new century approached, a transportation revolution was brewing. Visionary inventors and small companies, inspired by new technologies and driven by public outcry for relief from urban pollution, set out to remake an entire industry. Their goal was nothing less ambitious than the creation of a completely new transportation infrastructure.

One by one, the competing technologies fell by the wayside. Commercial experiments with electric batteries and even steam came and went. The winner? A nuisance byproduct of kerosene refining—gasoline. Cheap, plentiful, and easy to transport and dispense, its fast, hot flame made the internal-combustion engine practical. The burgeoning automobile industry provided people with unprecedented independence and vanquished one of the most serious pollution problems of its day—horse manure, 1,200 tons of it daily in New York City alone. Gasoline has dominated transportation for more than a century since. Its environmental, political, and social consequences, good and ill, have shaped our culture.

As this new century unfolds, we stand on the threshold of another transportation revolution: the transformation from petroleum to clean hydrogen power. Success depends on three critical elements. First, we must develop a clean, efficient, cost-effective hydrogen-fueled power source. Although an internal-combustion engine can burn hydrogen directly, the spotlight now focuses on electricity generated by proton-exchange-membrane (PEM) fuel cells. PEMs combine pure hydrogen fuel with oxygen from air with twice the energy efficiency of internal-combustion engines, and release only water vapor and heat as exhaust products. Second, the hydrogen revolution requires building an infrastructure to deliver hydrogen to the vehicle. And third, we need to find a means of storing useful quantities of hydrogen on-board vehicles.

Hydrogen vehicles can affect environmental cleanliness and energy independence only by entering the transportation mainstream; specialty and niche vehicles can make only incremental contributions at best. However, the uncompromised performance and reliability demanded by today's consumers mean that hydrogen fuel must offer the power, vehicle range, convenience, and affordability that people take for granted with gasoline. Only by more than satisfying the customer will hydrogen supplant gasoline.

This places tough requirements on the vehicular hydrogen-storage system (Figure 1 and table [in the original article]). One kilogram of hydrogen provides about the same chemical energy (142 MJ) as 1 gal of gasoline (131 MJ). Factoring in the greater efficiency of PEMs, we need to store about 1 kg of hydrogen for every 2 gal of gasoline on a similar internal-combustion-engine vehicle. For U.S. transportation, General Motors estimates that the entire onboard hydrogen fuel system—which includes the weight and volume of the hydrogen and its required fuel-delivery support such as the tank, pipes, pumps, and heat exchangers—must provide a volumetric energy density of at least 6 MJ/l and a gravimetric energy density of at least 6 MJ/kg energy equivalent of hydrogen to achieve significant market penetration. We will need about double those values to completely replace gasoline internal-combustion engines across the entire light-duty vehicle fleet.

These are system requirements; the hydrogen density, calculated from the weight and volume of the hydrogen alone (hydrogen basis) must be considerably higher to compensate for the weight and volume of the support hardware. Similarly, incorporating a hydride into an on-board storage system will substantially reduce its effective hydrogen density. There is no rule of thumb for the degree of reduction; it depends on the choice of storage medium and the required system design.

System safety is a given. Public perception and corporate citizenship will permit only an uncompromising attitude toward the safe implementation of a hydrogen economy. Fortunately, experts agree that hydrogen is inherently no more dangerous than gasoline, popular belief notwithstanding.

Storage Challenges

Compressed gaseous storage is closest to technical feasibility and is fundamentally appealing because of its familiarity and conceptual simplicity. The major difficulty with compressed hydrogen is its volume. One kilogram of hydrogen stored in common laboratory gas cylinders at 2,200 psi occupies 91.2 l (1.6 MJ/l, hydrogen basis—the effective energy density in a storage system will be substantially lower). For comparison, a mere 8.2 l of gasoline carries the same energy. Hydrogen tanks of 5,000 and 10,000 psi are being developed, but even at 10,000 psi, the volume of hydrogen is 27 l/kg (5.3 MJ/l, hydrogen basis).

At high pressures, deviations from the ideal gas law are large (Figure 2 [in the original article]). The hydrogen gas density at 10,000 psi is only two-thirds that of an ideal gas. Doubling the pressure to 20,000 psi, if that were technically feasible, would increase the gas density by only about 50%. High-pressure tanks are complex structures containing multiple layers for hydrogen confinement, rupture strength, and impact resistance. Furthermore, the tank must be cylindrical or near-cylindrical in shape, which seriously limits the options for tank placement on a vehicle. High-pressure storage is most appealing for large vehicles, such as buses, which have more available space—on the roof, for example.

Demonstration fuel-cell vehicles have been built using liquid-hydrogen storage. Here, the volumetric situation is somewhat improved compared to compressed gas because liquid hydrogen occupies about 14 l/kg (10 MJ/l, hydrogen basis). But hydrogen vaporizes at –253°C, which necessitates an exotic superinsulated cryogenic tank. Inevitably, heat leaking into the tank will produce serious boil-off, and the tank will begin to empty itself in days in undriven vehicles. Liquid hydrogen seems best suited to fleet applications, where vehicles return nightly to a central station for refueling. Advanced tank designs may extend the boil-off period to perhaps a few weeks. Proposals that combine high-pressure and cryogenic capabilities in a single tank design could also mitigate boil-off.

There is a large energy penalty for hydrogen compression (equal to 10 % of the energy content of the gas compressed) or liquefaction (30 %). Although this affects the storage economics, it does not impact the on-board storage system because the penalty is paid before the hydrogen is delivered to the vehicle.

Solid-Hydride Storage

Hydrogen can be chemically bound and stored as a solid compound. Solid-hydride storage materials release hydrogen gas under suitable conditions of temperature and hydrogen pressure (generally 2–5 bar) and, in some cases, in the presence of a further reactant. Solid hydrides can be loosely sorted into two groups:

- those for which the reverse hydriding reaction can be accomplished on-board the vehicle, generally by supplying hydrogen to the vehicle at a pressure higher than its working pressure, and

- those for which on-board rehydriding is impractical or impossible. In this case, refueling requires replacement of the storage medium itself, either by flush-and-fill or by exchanging the entire tank. The dehydrided material must then be recharged off-board; simply disposing of the spent material is unlikely to be economically or environmentally acceptable for mainstream transportation applications.

Perhaps the best-known solid-storage media for hydrogen are the reversible metal hydrides, such as lanthanum nickel hydride ($LaNi_5H_6$). Among the more hydrogenrich metal hydrides, volume is not the primary issue (Figure 3 [in the original article]). In fact, many hydrides, including $LaNi_5H_6$, store more hydrogen per unit volume than does liquid hydrogen. Furthermore, at modest hydrogen pressures (a few bars), $LaNi_5H_6$ releases hydrogen at or near room temperature. Its hydriding kinetics are also acceptable, and laboratory quantities can be dehydrided and rehydrided in 5 to 10 min. The main challenge of metal hydrides is their weight. Because the hydrogen content of $LaNi_5H_6$ is only 1.4% by weight (wt%), storing 5 kg of hydrogen would require 360 kg of $LaNi_5H_6$.

Some reversible metal hydrides store larger specific masses of hydrogen. Magnesium hydride (MgH_2) contains 7.6 wt% hydrogen (10.8 MJ/kg, based on material weight only, excluding the support hardware), a value that approaches feasible energy density. Regrettably, MgH_2 suffers from a thermodynamic obstacle common to high-capacity metal hydrides: the hydrogen is too strongly bound (Figure 4 [in the original article]). Its large enthalpy of hydride formation—the heat of formation $(\Delta H) = 37$ MJ/kg H2—has several important consequences. First, at the operating hydrogen pressure of the fuel cell (typically 2–5 bar), the hydrogen release temperature is commensurately high, nearly 300°C. Second, because dehydriding is endothermic, the ΔH must be supplied as heat to release the hydrogen. This represents nearly a 30% parasitic energy loss incurred on-board the vehicle. Finally, all of that heat is released again during fueling. Rapid fueling, say in 5 min, requires roughly 1 MW of cooling power to extract the heat energy from MgH_2. What we need is a new, as-yet-undiscovered, light-metal hydride with a hydrogen capacity greater than that of MgH_2 but with ΔH similar to that of $LaNi_5H_6$.

The solid hydride $NaAlH_4$ (sodium alanate) lies intermediate between the low- and high-temperature metal hydrides. It decomposes on heating in two steps, first to sodium aluminum hydride (Na_3AlH_6) plus aluminum, and subsequently to sodium hydride (NaH) plus additional aluminum. (Further decomposition of the NaH requires impractically high temperatures for PEM fuel-cell applications.) The combined theoretical hydrogen capacity is 5.6 wt% (7.8 MJ/kg, material weight only). Incorporating titanium, or titanium and zirconium dopants, has yielded experimental dehydriding rates of 1 wt%/h at 110 and 160°C for the first and second decomposition steps, respectively, but at the cost of lower hydrogen capacity (~ 4.5 wt%). Even relatively slow rehydriding requires high hydrogen pressure (~ 80 bar).

A new storage material based on transformations between a series of lithium–nitrogen–hydrogen compounds has been identified recently. Although interesting, this system still suffers from a relatively high ΔH and a modest hydrogen capacity of only 6.5 wt%.

Nonreversible hydrides can store and release hydrogen. Sodium borohydride ($NaBH_4$) and NaH are examples of hydrolysis hydrides; adding water releases hydrogen and forms sodium metaborate ($NaBO_2$) or sodium

hydroxide (NaOH). Although these materials generate considerable quantities of hydrogen, on-board system problems such as thermal control are significant, and off-board regeneration infrastructure and energy-efficiency considerations remain challenging.

Carbon Nanomaterials

Since 1997, numerous reports in the technical literature and news releases have claimed that carbon nanofibers, nanotubes, and similar carbon nanostructures can sorb anywhere from 3 to 67 wt % hydrogen at room temperature. Most claims require hydrogen pressures of around 100 bar, but in a few cases, researchers claim high hydrogen capacity at ambient pressure. Although it is widely accepted that carbon nanotubes in 120-bar hydrogen gas can sorb up to 8 wt % hydrogen at *cryogenic* temperatures by simple physisorption, the binding energy is far too low to account for high hydrogen storage at room temperature. The amount of hydrogen physisorbed on activated carbon, for example, drops by an order of magnitude between 77 K and room temperature, to 0.7 wt % or less. Hydrogen capacities approaching 8 wt % (1 hydrogen atom/carbon atom) at room temperature would require a currently unknown carbon–hydrogen bonding mechanism intermediate in strength between physisorption and chemisorption.

Worldwide efforts to verify large hydrogen storage in nanostructured carbon have met with no real success. A few claims have been proven wrong (but nevertheless continue to be cited in the technical literature). Many "demonstrations" of hydrogen sorption rely on measurement of the drop in hydrogen pressure with time in a "leak-free" sample vessel. This technique appears simple but is deceptively vulnerable to error. Cooling of the hydrogen gas after pressurization can easily masquerade as sorption, and hydrogen is notorious for leaking. It cannot be overemphasized: there is no substitute for careful, deliberate research conducted using accurate techniques and with a full appreciation of the possible pitfalls.

It remains difficult to dismiss all such claims as spurious, and new, unverified claims continue to appear regularly. Hope persists that carbon nanomaterials might prove viable for hydrogen storage. Nevertheless, the early euphoria has largely given way to a more skeptical view of its prospects. For now, we have no independently verified evidence of technologically significant hydrogen sorption at room temperature.

Conclusion

The dawn of a hydrogen economy for mainstream vehicles may well depend on breakthrough research to find new storage materials or innovative storage concepts. To this end, the U.S. Department of Energy has issued what it calls a Grand Challenge for the research and development of hydrogen storage materials and technologies and has committed $150 million to it over the next five years. Only by answering this challenge can hydrogen take its place as the transportation fuel of the future.

Thus far, most of the papers in this text have covered theoretical ideas that somewhat foretell the future. A perpetual motion machine, for example, has been dreamt up by scientists but is not available in the marketplace yet. If the past is any indication of the future, then many theories will eventually lead to producible consumer goods.

This article describes technology that is very much in the here and now. Note that it was written for auto and truck specialists. They have some understanding of mechanics, but the article assumes little prior knowledge of physics and thermodynamics. For this reason, the piece provides a good introduction on how basic refrigerator and air-conditioning systems work.

While cooling systems now are commonplace, they puzzled researchers less than a century ago. In fact, renowned physicist Albert Einstein spent much of the latter part of his career trying to design a better refrigerator. Fast-forward beyond Einstein and the science described in this article, and you might find cooling units built from specially designed semi-conductor materials using quantum mechanical theory. Already, the military is testing such a device on its shipboard generators. This article also provides a good overview on how kitchen refrigerators and car air-conditioning systems work. —JV

"Air Conditioning Theory and Policies"
by Bob Freudenberger
Auto and Truck International, July/August 1999

Believe it or not, there were attempts to chill the passenger compartment before refrigeration was invented—or even the automobile! In 1884, Englishman William Whiteley placed blocks of ice in a tray under a horse carriage and used a fan attached to a wheel to force air inside. Later, a bucket of ice in front of a floor vent became the automotive equivalent.

Since the U.S.A. includes areas that are much hotter than the northern European countries where a large number of other advancements in automotive technology were developed, it is not surprising that the first car with real air conditioning was the 1939 Packard. The huge evaporator was mounted in the trunk, leaving little room for luggage, and the only way to shut it off was to stop, raise the hood, and remove the compressor belt. It was, however, a true refrigeration system. Cadillac followed in 1941.

Today, most of the cars in operation throughout the world are equipped with air conditioning. So, it is

important for anyone involved in auto service to have a clear idea of how this system operates and the best way to handle service. This article is intended to provide both.

Thermodynamics

Our use of the word "thermodynamics" may intimidate you, but a little physics is a necessary basis for an understanding of refrigeration. Besides, the principles are not difficult to grasp, and you already know some of them from experience.

To begin with, heat is energy, and cold is the absence of heat. Due to molecular movement, all substances contain heat in some degree. Scientists have figured that –273.15 degrees C (–459.67 degrees F) is absolute zero, where no heat whatsoever is present, but they have never been able to achieve this theoretical state.

Now we come to the thermodynamic law that explains how any refrigeration unit—or any heating unit, for that matter—works: Heat always moves from a warmer object to a colder object. When you put ice cubes in your drink, the liquid do not pick up coldness from the ice. Instead, the heat that the liquid contains travels into the ice so that the drink loses heat and the ice gains it.

Heat can always be caused to move by creating a temperature differential between two objects or substances. The energy will travel from the warm object into the cold one until both their temperatures are equal.

In an air conditioner, then, cold does not radiate from the evaporator. Rather, the heat in the air inside the car travels through the evaporator coils into the refrigerant, which carries it to the condenser where it dissipates as if trying to heat up the atmosphere.

The quantity of heat, by the way, is usually measured in calories kilocalories (kcal), or British Thermal Units (BTUs). One kcal is the amount of energy required to raise the temperature of one kilogram of water one degree C at sea level, and one BTU is the quantity of work that will increase the temperature of one pound of water one degree Fahrenheit, also at sea level.

Change of State

The greatest amount of heat movement to or from a substance occurs when it changes its state, as from a solid to a liquid when ice melts. The changes of state we are interested in here, however, are from a liquid to a gas, which is called evaporation, and from a gas to a liquid, which is known as condensation. Both require the movement of a tremendous quantity of calories or BTUs.

If you have one kilogram of water at 100 deg. C (or, one pound of water at 212 deg. F) in a container at sea level, it will soak up an almost unbelievable amount of heat without getting any hotter. Instead of the one kcal needed at lower temperatures to raise it one degree C (or, the one BTU to raise one lb. one deg. F), 540 kcal (or, 970 BTUs) will have to be added in order to change the water to vapor. In other words, you can burn a house down around the container and that water will not go above 100 deg. C (212 deg. F) until it has changed into a gas. You have added a great deal of heat to the water, but you cannot locate it with a thermometer.

This is what is known as the latent heat of vaporization—the abnormally large amount of heat a liquid can absorb when changing state without getting any warmer. The vapor will hold this energy until it condenses, at which time it will release it.

Of course, water is not used in automotive air conditioning systems. Instead, a synthetic chemical refrigerant does the job. For five decades, the Standard refrigerant was dichlorodifluoromethane, also known as R-12 or Freon. But this chemical was found to do serious damage to the earth's ozone layer, so we now have a more environmentally friendly refrigerant, R-134a, which has been accepted by all auto makers as standard.

Both refrigerants have much lower freezing and vaporization points than water, but they still absorb large quantities of heat when evaporated and release it when they condense. Liquid refrigerant in an auto air conditioner absorbs heat from the passenger compartment as it changes to a vapor in the evaporator. This gas then gives off the same amount of heat to the outside air as it turns back into a liquid in the condenser.

In Cars

The automotive air conditioner is a mechanical system designed to move heat. The two most common A/C designs are the thermostatic expansion valve type and the cycling clutch orifice tube, or CCOT, type. We will cover the expansion valve system first, then explain the differences between that and CCOT.

Every air conditioner has both a high-pressure and a low-pressure section. The high pressure side includes the discharge side of the compressor, the condenser, the receiver/drier, the inlet half of the thermostatic expansion valve, and the necessary hoses and connections. The low pressure side comprises the suction side of the compressor, the evaporator, and the outlet half of the expansion valve.

The parts that work together to accomplish heat transfer deserve some explanation. The heart of the system is the compressor. Although there are several types, all are belt-driven through an electromagnetic clutch and move refrigerant by means of pistons or scrolls and one-way valves.

The compressor's basic purpose is to squeeze the low pressure refrigerant vapor it receives from the evaporator. This concentrates the heat in the vapor, thus raising its temperature. This happens because of another law of physics that states that when a gas is compressed, its temperature goes up.

The idea here is to make the vapor hotter than the atmosphere so that while it is in the condenser it will dissipate the heat it carries. The compressor's other job is to circulate sufficient refrigerant through the system. An important point to remember is that these pumps are designed to move only vapor. If liquid refrigerant gets into them it is apt to break the valves or cause the pistons to lock up.

The next component in line is the condenser, which is on the high pressure side of the system and is mounted in front of the radiator. It is a series of tubes covered with fins to aid in heat dissipation. It receives heat-laden high-pressure refrigerant from the compressor. The hot vapor gives off most of its heat during the change to a high-pressure warm liquid.

The liquid then makes its way to the receiver/drier, which is basically a storage reservoir that can supply the evaporator with the amount of refrigerant needed at any particular time. It also serves to remove and retain foreign particles and moisture from the refrigerant by means of a filter and a dehydrating or desiccant agent, usually silica alumina.

It is important that moisture be removed from the system because drops of it may collect and freeze in the thermal expansion valve orifice, blocking the flow to the evaporator, and also because water reacts with refrigerant to form various acids, which will rot the system from the inside out.

Since the drying substance can absorb only so much moisture before it becomes saturated, the receiver/drier needs to be replaced once in a while. Traditionally, this was recommended every third time the system was opened.

A metering device known as a thermostatic expansion valve is the next recipient of the refrigerant. Its job is to control the flow to the evaporator so that maximum cooling results, and to assure complete vaporization of the refrigerant in the coils, eliminating the possibility of liquid getting into the compressor. It does this by means of a variable orifice, which opens and closes according to the heat load. Refrigerant enters the valve as a warm, high-pressure liquid and leaves it as a cold, low-pressure atomized liquid.

This cold spray then shoots into the evaporator, which is simply a refrigeration coil inside the passenger compartment, where it picks up huge volumes of heat as it vaporizes. The temperature of the refrigerant is lower than that of the air inside the car, so heat just follows its natural inclination to flow from a warm substance to a cooler one and the passengers get relief from a scorching summer day.

The refrigerant will be many degrees warmer at the outlet of the evaporator than it was at the inlet and its volume will be greater.

From here, the refrigerant goes to the low-pressure side of the compressor and the cycle starts over.

Of course, this is a very basic A/C system, but it does include everything necessary to produce a cooling effect.

CCOT

The cycling clutch orifice tube, or CCOT, system is somewhat different. In the first place, instead of a receiver/drier, it uses an accumulator. This device is similar to a receiver/drier in function, but is mounted downstream of the evaporator on the suction side of the compressor instead of upstream of the thermostatic expansion valve.

In place of the thermostatic expansion valve, CCOT systems use a fixed orifice tube to meter the refrigerant into the evaporator. By itself, this would result in evaporator freeze-up because there would be no way to control the amount of cooling as there is with an expansion valve.

So, CCOT systems use a pressure cycling switch to energize and de energize the compressor clutch, thus controlling the amount of refrigerant the compressor is pumping through the system and regulating the temperature. This switch is normally screwed into the accumulator and turns on and off at preset pressures.

Old or New?

As of this writing, most manufacturers and other authorities say you should keep systems designed for R-12 Freon running on Freon as long as that is legal and economically feasible.

Making whatever repair is necessary, then recharging with R-12 will assure like-new performance and keep labor costs down. For now, that is. If the vehicle's owner plans to keep it for years, the next time it loses its charge Freon may be fabulously expensive or perhaps not available at all at any cost.

Going to R-134a, on the other hand, is no longer considered an experimental procedure fraught with unforeseen pitfalls. It is done all the time and the results are usually fine provided you do it right, which includes making sure you inject enough of the proper synthetic compressor oil, draw down a deep vacuum for 45 minutes or more to take out a little moisture (you will never get all that much by vacuuming) and those performance-robbing NCGs (Non-Condensable Gases, essentially air), and preferably replace the receiver/drier or accumulator (fresh desiccant will take care of the H_2O evacuation cannot get).

After retrofit, future repairs will be relatively inexpensive because this new refrigerant will be the standard for as long as we care to speculate, assuring a plentiful and cheap supply, and you can be certain everybody in the service business will have the equipment and knowledge to handle it.

You had better be very sure, however, that your customer understands that while R-134a gives satisfactory performance in most cases, there is a good chance he will notice that his A/C will not cool down as fast or feel as ice-cold as it did on Freon.

Lube It

The refrigerant oil issue of PAG (polyalkyline glycol) versus POE (polyolester) is a volatile one, so suffice it to say here that you absolutely must install a sufficient amount of one or the other synthetic lubricant during retrofit or the compressor will burn out. It is an unfortunate fact that R-134a simply cannot transport the droplets of mineral oil that the pump needs for continuous lubrication, so it will end up dry. Speaking of dry, we should mention that at the 1999 Mobile Air Conditioning Society International convention, some compressor makers and remanufacturers said that in cases where they ship units dry, they often get them back as returns STILL dry. Also, there is no problem leaving the mineral oil in the system when you convert to R-134a and one of the new lubricants. The worst you will be risking is a one to two percent reduction in heat exchange efficiency.

Reprinted with permission from Adams Business Media.

The human body, like any machine, can collapse if too much heat disrupts normal functions. Dehydration, heat stroke, and even death can occur if an individual is exposed to too much heat for too long of a period without some form of relief. In the Western world, we rely heavily upon fossil fuel–run cooling systems, such as electric air conditioners. In other parts of the world, where such technologies are not as readily available to the average citizen, alternative forms of coping have evolved with minimal investment of time and money, and less damage to the environment.

One of the most clever and simplest techniques used by residents of Bangkok is found in the design of their homes. As you will read, Thai builders took the basic principle that heat rises and moves from hotter to colder areas to construct homes. Slats are built into roofs to release hot air, while cooler air is let in at another area. Floor materials consist of wood and tile, which tend to be poor conductors of heat.

While we do not all live in cities that are exposed to such prolonged periods of hot weather, lessons can be learned from the people of Bangkok's ability to adapt. In the state of California, for example, builders finally have realized over the decades that it is best to avoid *placing structures directly over earthquake faults as a means of minimizing potential damage. Sometimes the most simple, obvious solutions produce the greatest gains. —JV*

"Living with Heat: How Do Residents Cope with the Sweltering Heat and Humidity in Bangkok—Dubbed the Hottest City in the World?"
by Mace Bentley
Weatherwise, **January/February 2004**

The sky was painted the milky blue shade of the humid tropics as my flight approached Bangkok. A veil of wispy cirrus clouds dotted the sky. As we descended through 5,500 meters (18,046 feet), the outside temperature climbed above 0° Celsius (32° Fahrenheit). For the freezing level to be that high, the atmosphere below had to be layer upon layer of air bulging with heat all the way to the ground.

Bangkok (Krungthepmahanakorn in Thai), Thailand, is a mix of dense jungle, modern buildings, and sprawling suburbs. The city, home to more than 10 million people, has earned the dubious honor of being called the Hottest City in the World by the World Meteorological Organization. At the airport, the air temperature was 93° Fahrenheit (34° Celsius) and the dew point was 82° Fahrenheit (28° Celsius), yielding a midday relative humidity of 71 percent. Yet, this was undoubtedly cooler than downtown Bangkok, and it was still hours before the hottest part of the day. Bangkok was definitely living up to its hot reputation.

The apparent temperature, also known as the heat index, indicates the stress on the body as humidity slows the shedding of excess heat. On this morning, it was 115° Fahrenheit (46° Celsius). In the United States, if the apparent temperature is expected to exceed 105° Fahrenheit (41° Celsius) for just three hours, the National Weather Service issues a Heat Advisory. Bangkok exceeds this threshold every afternoon—for more than six unrelenting months each year.

The human body experiences immense stress trying to survive in these conditions. Sweat becomes the currency of cooling. In each drop of sweat, molecules bang into one another at a mind-boggling rate. Through collisions, some molecules gain enough speed to break free of the attractive forces of neighboring molecules and carry energy (heat) away from the body. This evaporation allows our bodies to cool down. But, at the same time, vapor molecules are crashing back to the sweat droplets, returning heat to the body.

Like a checking account, there are withdrawals, i.e., evaporation, and deposits, i.e., condensation. If the outgoing exceeds the incoming, the body cools. On a humid day, more vapor molecules are zipping about than on a less humid day. Therefore, there are more deposits; the rate of cooling slows and body heat accumulates. Unlike a bank, when the account balance grows in the world of cooling, trouble looms.

Worldwide, it is thought that more people die each year from the effects of excessive heat than the combined effects of tornadoes, floods, and blizzards. When the apparent temperature passes 100° Fahrenheit (42° Celsius) and continues to rise, that weak-in-the-knees feeling progresses to heat exhaustion, then on to potentially fatal heat stroke.

In July 1995, a heat wave descended on Chicago. From the 10th through the 16th temperatures exceeded 90° Fahrenheit (32° Celsius) at Chicago's Midway Airport. The level of stifling heat was not only uncomfortable, it was deadly; more than 500 people died. The heat-related deaths centered on the elderly, who stayed indoors without air-conditioning and with windows tightly shut. Sadly, a similar pattern unfolded in Paris this summer.

In the wake of the 1995 heat wave, Chicago implemented a plan that declares a heat emergency if the combined effects of heat and humidity create an apparent temperature of at least 105° Fahrenheit. Expect to see similar efforts throughout Europe following this past summer's heat wave that cost the continent an estimated 16,000 lives.

In a city perpetually plagued by heat and humidity, why doesn't hot weather hog the headlines? Unlike Chicago, which receives only occasional visits by the deadly duo of heat and humidity, the citizens of Bangkok endure oppressive conditions for more than six months each year. Although many businesses have air-conditioning, most homes do not.

So how do the citizens of Bangkok cope with the hottest city in the world? During the hottest time of the year, and just about every other day for that matter, the spirit of mai pen rai ("don't worry about it") guides most Thai people. They move on and make the best of it.

Most of the city's residents jokingly agree that Bangkok has three seasons; "hot, hotter, and hottest." Hot season runs from November until February when high temperatures reach the upper 80s (31° Celsius) and lows drop to the upper 60s (19° Celsius). This is a popular time of year to enjoy the city's numerous outdoor cafes and concerts.

May through October is the hotter season when temperatures hover in the low-to-mid 90s (34° Celsius). Although temperatures are not at their peak, the addition of high humidity makes life rather uncomfortable. The apparent temperature commonly reaches levels above 110° Fahrenheit (43° Celsius); a suffocating mix of heat, humidity, and pollution makes it a challenge to venture outside. Also during the hotter season, southwesterly winds, part of the better-known Indian Monsoon, carry moisture from the Gulf of Thailand and Andaman Sea. The hot days and abundant moisture give birth to thunderstorms; the almost daily afternoon showers bring an eagerly anticipated short spell of relief.

During the hottest season, Bangkok's climate pushes the limits of human endurance. Commencing in late February, high temperatures reach the upper 90s (36 Celsius) and lows only dip to the upper 70s (25° Celsius). It is at this time of year that Bangkok becomes almost unlivable. Many Thai people simply run from one air-conditioned building to another.

Heat is a constant in Bangkok. "We don't pay much attention to the weather forecast," a Bangkok acquaintance said, "because we know what the weather will be like—hot!"

From clothing to their overall outlook on life, Thais adapt. Many wear western attire, but with an emphasis on linen, cotton, and loose fitting garments to beat the heat. Traditional Thai clothing is even more comfortable such as the gang geng-lay, a popular large cotton casual pant worn by both men and women. Many older Thais do not wear shorts, but they are becoming popular among the younger generation, and sandals are the norm for many.

Housing construction also respects the hot environment. Many Thai houses have either wood or ceramic tile floors that stay cooler than carpet—a pleasant feel to the feet since Thais always remove their shoes before going inside. In America, summer is barbecuing season. In Thailand, it is always grilling season, since the cooking range is typically outside the kitchen door. Baking is rare in Thai homes; the heat of an oven, added to the already unbearable atmosphere, makes baking nearly impossible. Another surprise to American visitors is that sinks usually have only one handle, since most Thai houses do not have hot water. But after touring Bangkok for one day, a cool shower makes sense.

Traditional Thai teak houses offer other climatic adaptations. Rising hot air escapes through vents placed high in the eaves of the steeply pitched roofs and is replaced by cooler night air pulled in from the outside at lower levels. Many older Thai houses were built on stilts, a number of feet off the ground, to intercept any breezes that may develop in the afternoon. After visiting several of these houses during the blazingly hot afternoon, I am happy to report that the design worked; the inside was considerably cooler than expected.

Because home air conditioning is rare in Bangkok, city dwellers have developed creative substitutes like placing a bowl of ice in front of a fan or sleeping on the cooler ceramic tile or wood floors. One Thai friend, fondly recalling her childhood in southern Thailand said, "During the summer I remember many nights sleeping on the floor and waking up the next morning in a puddle of sweat."

Another way to avoid the heat is in air-conditioned malls, which are usually crowded with those wanting a brief respite from the heat and humidity.

Because Thais celebrate the New Year on April 13 when the weather is typically the hottest, the new beginning is welcomed with a national water festival. No one outdoors is safe from the soaking relief of a water balloon or water cannon.

Even car design yields to the omnipresent heat. Most cars and all taxis have air conditioning. A Thai car dealer told me that the first thing the dealers do when they receive a shipment of new cars is to take out the factory-installed air conditioning and install one made in Thailand. The factory air conditioning just isn't strong enough.

Although all Thais complain about the heat and humidity, they remain a vibrant, functioning society with low rates of violent crime and depression. During periods of intense heat in the United States, violence and depression become headline issues.

How does someone live happily ever after in the world's hottest city with 10 million others? By learning not to worry about things they can't change and concentrating on those that they can—a salient piece of advice when faced with a heat index of 115° Fahrenheit.

Weatherwise, Vol. 57, Issue 1, p. 16, Jan/Feb 2004. Reprinted with permission of the Helen Dwight Reid Educational Foundation. Published by Heldref Publications, 1319 Eighteenth St., NW, Washington, DC 20036-1802. Copyright © 2004.

Most science students have conducted simple lab experiments to demonstrate basic laws of science. These experiments help us to better understand scientific principles, but often they hold no other usage outside of the classroom setting. Here is an invention that mirrors such experiments in its simplicity and ability to exemplify science laws, but it also could help millions of people to cope with heat in desert communities. Best of all, as the author of the first article points out, the device requires only a thirty-cent investment and needs no expensive fuel to operate.

The principle behind the device is the same used to cool the human body. When we sweat, moisture on the skin evaporates and releases heat, thus cooling the body down. Here, water within dampened sand evaporates and cools down a pot. Since the cooling system can be plunked down anywhere and can be easily transported and constructed out of readily available materials, it might make a viable solution for

desert dwellers and people who must travel across desert areas without benefit of refrigeration or even a plastic cooler. Nomads who transport camels or other work animals from one site to another, for example, might find the idea useful. Similar to the solutions Bangkok residents developed for coping with the heat, Mohammed Bah Abba has found a very clever and environmentally friendly way of dealing with the potentially deadly problem of heat. These two selections—the second, a Rolex Awards profile of Abba, whom the association honored— chronicle Abba's achievement. —JV

"Desert Fridge: Cooling Foods When There's Not a Socket Around"
by Naomi Lubick
Scientific American, **November 19, 2000**

Thanks to the second law of thermodynamics, Mohammed Bah Abba has developed a refrigerator that doesn't need electricity. What's more, it costs 30 cents to make.

The elegant design consists of an earthenware pot nestled inside a larger pot, packed with a layer of damp sand. When the "Pot-in-Pot" system is stored in a very dry, well-ventilated place, the water held in the pots' clay walls and sand evaporates, carrying heat with it. The inner pot therefore cools down—and makes a useful refrigerator in the northern deserts of Nigeria, where Abba lives and works. Abba says his trials showed that tomatoes would last several weeks instead of several days and that African spinach (amaranth), which normally wilts within hours of harvest, can last up to 12 days. (He's never measured, though, just how many degrees cooler the inner pot becomes.)

Abba's fridge provides an alternative for desert cultures, which generally dry their foods to preserve them. Drying doesn't diminish protein or calorie content much, notes William R. Leonard, a biological anthropologist at Northwestern University who has worked in the high desert of the Peruvian altiplano. "But things like vitamin C are likely to be in shorter supply" in the dried foods, Leonard says. In addition, some foods, such as spinach and onions, cannot be dried, remarks Abba, a lecturer at Jigawa State Polytechnic in Dutse, Nigeria. The Pot-in-Pot may have a great social impact, too: Abba says that young girls who used it would not have to sell their families' freshly picked foods right away and thus would have time to go to school.

For his work, Abba received one of five biennial Rolex Awards for Enterprise on September 27. The others were Elizabeth Nicholls, a Canadian paleontologist who unearthed an ichthyosaur in British Columbia; Maria Eliza Manteca Oñate, an Ecuadorian environmentalist promoting sustainable farming in the Andes; Laurent Pordié, a French ethnopharmacologist who is preserving traditional Tibetan healing methods in northern India; and David Schweidenback, an American recovering used bicycles in the U.S. for shipment to developing countries (see www.rolexawards.com).

Mohammed Bah Abba
Rolexawards.com

Manufacture and supply an innovative earthenware cooling system to preserve perishable foods in developing countries with arid climates

Northern Nigeria is an impoverished region where people in rural communities eke out a living from subsistence farming. With no electricity, and therefore no refrigeration, perishable foods spoil within days. Such spoilage causes disease and loss of income for needy farmers, who are forced to sell their produce daily. Nigerian teacher Mohammed Bah Abba was motivated by his concern for the rural poor and by his interest in indigenous African technology to seek a practical, local solution to these problems. His extremely simple and inexpensive earthenware "pot-in-pot" cooling device, based on a principle of physics already known in ancient Egypt, is revolutionising lives in this semi-desert area.

The art of pottery is deeply rooted in African culture. In northern Nigeria, earthenware pots have been used since ancient times as cooking and water storage vessels, coffins, wardrobes and banks. Today, these clay pots are almost extinct, replaced by aluminium containers and more modern methods of burying the dead, storing clothes and saving money.

Born in 1964 into a family of pot makers and raised in the rural north, Mohammed Bah Abba was familiar from an early age with the various practical and symbolic uses of traditional clay pots, and learned as a child the rudiments of pottery. Subsequently studying biology, chemistry and geology at school, he unravelled the technical puzzle that led him years later to develop the "pot-in-pot preservation/cooling system."

He was selected as a Rolex Laureate in 2000 for this ingenious technique that requires no external energy supply to preserve fruit, vegetables and other perishables in hot, arid climates. The pot-in-pot cooling system, a kind of "desert refrigerator," helps subsistence farmers by reducing food spoilage and waste and thus increasing their income and limiting the health hazards of decaying foods. Abba says he developed the pot-in-pot "to help the rural poor in a cost-effective, participatory and sustainable way."

The pot-in-pot consists of two earthenware pots of different diameters, one placed inside the other. The space between the two pots is filled with wet sand that is kept constantly moist, thereby keeping both pots damp. Fruit, vegetables and other items such as soft drinks are put in the smaller inner pot, which is covered with a damp cloth. The phenomenon that occurs is based on a simple principle of physics: the water contained in the sand between the two pots evaporates towards the outer surface of the larger pot where the drier outside air is circulating. By virtue of the laws of thermodynamics, the evaporation process automatically causes a drop in temperature of several degrees, cooling the inner container, destroying harmful micro-organisms and preserving the perishable foods inside.

The principle of physics used by the pot-in-pot is present in nature itself. A panting dog, for example, uses the same process, losing heat through its tongue. It is also well known by humans in arid countries. Indeed, the roots of innovation spread wide and deep, and Abba's pot-in-pot is one of several ingenious applications of cooling by evaporation.

The city of Qena in Upper Egypt is renowned for its porous-clay cooling vessels—a tradition spanning more than three millennia. In Burkina Faso, the Jula people's traditional jars are sometimes soaked in water before goods are stored in them, so that they stay cool by evaporation. This single-pot design is similar to the pot-in-pot, but less efficient.

In India, street vendors often cool fruit or drinks for their customers by suspending bags of produce in a porous clay container. Also in India, a rectangular enclosure of wet bricks is used to preserve foodstuffs from heat. Water seeps slowly through the porous bricks, evaporating from the surface and keeping the entire structure cool. The Pundjab Agricultural University in Ludhiana has recently tested an improved version of this system, which is closer to the pot-in-pot than any other device. It uses double-brick walls, with wet sand between them. The sand is kept wet, and the entire chamber is covered with a moist mat. Fruit and vegetables inside the chamber are maintained at temperatures below 20° C.

In 1992, laboratory experiments to measure the temperature drop in a two-pot design, where a small clay receptacle is placed within another receptacle filled with water, were carried out at the University of Benin City by Nigerian professor Victor Aimiuwu. He found that the device had good cooling properties, remaining up to 14 degrees cooler than the surrounding environment.

Still, among all the similar devices and traditional cooling pots, there is nothing quite like the pot-in-pot with its unique combination of simplicity and effectiveness. In fact, the Nigerian teacher's project shows how, for the Rolex Awards, originality is far more than a bright idea—it means turning an inspiration into a concrete achievement with a major impact.

"Mohammed Bah Abba won a Rolex Award not simply because he designed the pot-in-pot. He overcame obstacles to produce and distribute it, and also ensured that it could be bought for an affordable price by the people who need it," says Rebecca Irvin, head of the Rolex Awards Secretariat in Geneva.

To understand the relevance of Abba's Rolex Award-winning project, it is necessary to look at the geography of northern Nigeria and the restricted lives led by the people. This region is primarily a semi-desert scrubland inhabited by a large, mostly agriculture-based population, the majority of whom live in abject poverty. Polygamy is a dominant feature of the family structure, and women, living in purdah, are confined to their homes and seriously disadvantaged in terms of health care, education and employment opportunities. Young girls are particularly enslaved because they are forced to go out each day and rapidly sell food that would otherwise perish, in order to add to the meagre family income.

A key reason for the pot-in-pot's success is the lack of electricity in most of the northern rural communities, for without electricity there can be no refrigeration.

Even in towns and cities the power supply is erratic. Most of the urban poor cannot even afford refrigerators.

In the context of an economically drained nation facing severe communication, transport and utility problems, Abba set out to try and help improve the ailing economy. He became a lecturer in business studies at Jigawa State Polytechnic in Dutse in 1990. When not teaching, Abba serves as a consultant to the regional United Nations Development Programme (UNDP) in Jigawa, organising community activities and giving seminars. A staunch supporter of women's rights, he is also a consultant with the state's Ministry for Women Affairs and Social Mobilization.

These consultancies brought Abba in close contact with rural communities, where he observed the extreme hardships suffered by subsistence farmers and their families. "Through these observations, I became motivated to revitalise earthen pot usage and extend the life of perishable foods," he explains.

Abba's first trials of the pot-in-pot proved successful. Eggplants, for example, stayed fresh for 27 days instead of three, and tomatoes and peppers lasted for three weeks or more. African spinach, which usually spoils after a day, remained edible after 12 days in the pot-in-pot.

The enterprising teacher persistently refined his invention for two years between 1995 and 1997. He then tapped into the large unemployed local workforce and hired skilled pot makers to mass produce the first batch of 5,000 pot-in-pots. Manufacturing these devices at his own expense, he began distributing them for free to five villages in Jigawa. For this initial phase of his project, he received limited financial backing from his brother and assistance in the form of transportation, fuel and labour from the UNDP, the regional government, a local women's development group and the Jigawa State Polytechnic.

In 1999, Abba supplied another dozen local villages with 7,000 pots, again at his expense. Sold for between US$2 for the smaller pot-in-pots and US$4 for the bigger version, the pot-in-pot stays affordable, while proceeds from sales help finance manufacturing and distribution costs.

However, one of the biggest obstacles faced by the project was educating the villagers about this simple technology. Abba devised an educational campaign tailored to village life and the illiterate population, featuring a video-recorded play by local actors who dramatise the benefits of the desert refrigerator. Abba began showing the video in villages using a makeshift cloth screen and a portable projector and generator. "Nightfall is best," he comments, "because this is when farmers head home and are keen to watch an entertaining presentation."

Thanks to a "very timely" Rolex Award, Abba has been able to distribute pot-in-pots in 11 northern Nigerian states, and further his expansion plans in other countries such as Cameroon, Niger, Chad and the Democratic Republic of Congo.

In 2002, with Abba's approval, the Intermediate Technology Development Group (ITDG) and the University of Al Fashir carried out experiments in Sudan to assess the performances of the pot-in-pot in food conservation. The excellent results led the Women's Association for Earthenware Manufacturing in Darfur to manufacture their own pot-in-pots, called zeer in Arabic.

As of early 2005, Abba had distributed a total of 91,795 pot-in-pots. "My life has greatly changed since receiving the Rolex Award," he says.

And the future is bright. The Nigerian Laureate has been asked to help introducing and adapting his cooling device in Eritrea, where it could preserve insulin vials for diabetic patients in remote rural areas, India, Haiti and Honduras.

The impact of the pot-in-pot on individuals' lives is overwhelming. "Farmers are now able to sell on demand rather than 'rush sell' because of spoilage," says Abba, "and income levels have noticeably risen. Married women also have an important stake in the process, as they can sell food from their homes and overcome their age-old dependency on their husbands as the sole providers." In turn and, perhaps most significantly for the advancement of the female population, Abba's invention liberates girls from having to hawk food each day. Instead, they are now free to attend school and the number of girls enrolling in village primary schools is rising.

These factors, coupled with the effect that the pot-in-pot has had in stemming disease, are, in Abba's words, making "the pot-in-pot a tangible and exciting solution to a severe local problem."

Well known for his dedication, Abba is also praised for his concern with the social and economic development of his fellow Nigerians. "Mr Abba cares for the progress of society in general," says Mrs Hadiza Abdulwahab, president of the local Society for Women Empowerment and Development.

The permanent secretary of the State Ministry of Women Affairs and Social Mobilization, Mrs Rabi Umar, agrees. She believes that Abba has been "selfless and tireless" in his efforts to make his project succeed. Summing up his work, she says: "The pot-in-pot project is the first to use simple cultural solutions to address the primary needs of the rural northern Nigerian population, for whom the basic necessities of life are nearly non-existent."

Reprinted with permission from the Rolex Awards for Enterprise.

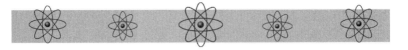

The next time you stay at a hotel, Big Brother might be watching, but in this case, the watchdog is an electronic device that controls the thermodynamics of the room. Consider how expensive it is to heat or cool an average apartment or house using a heater and air-conditioning unit. Hotels must absorb the cost of controlling temperatures in each room because guests can control how hot or cold their space is.

New technology has enabled an electronic energy management system to regulate temperatures and the usage of heating/cooling units within each hotel room. The creator of the system, a company called Senercomm, states that guests' comfort will not be compromised if the units are centrally manipulated during times of peak usage and when the desired indoor temperature strays too far from the outside ambient temperature.

Senercomm claims the system could lower utility usage by up to 45 percent. Hotel and motel managers, for whom this article was written, will then have to weigh the start-up and maintenance costs for the system versus the long-term savings. The system is similar to solar devices in that they sometimes have higher start-up costs but yield greater savings over time. —JV

"Energy-Management Systems Provide More Than Savings"
by John Jesitus
Hotel & Motel Management, June 18, 2001

With power prices increasing throughout the country, hoteliers are looking more closely at cutting energy consumption wherever possible. New energy-management systems can accomplish this goal without compromising guest satisfaction, while also adding features that virtually were unthinkable a few years ago.

Along with lowering utility usage by as much as 45 percent, current energy-management technology can increase guests' comfort and safety through functions such as informing staff if guests have left rooms unlocked.

With fossil-fuel prices rising by as much as 40 percent in some markets, hoteliers' main concern is curbing these runaway costs.

"As a result, there's a huge push for energy-management products for the guestroom," said Larry Gomez, president and owner of Senercomm. "This is an area owners and operators have been aware of for years, but there really hasn't been a significant push or need in the past for them to make that kind of investment."

"For more than 90 percent of the country, energy-management systems that control heating, ventilation and air conditioning are the single largest thing hotels can do to reduce energy costs, of which between 25 percent and 90 percent are attributable to guestrooms," said Duane Buckingham, president and c.e.o. of INNCOM International.

Similar to systems from Senercomm and Lodging Technology Corp., INNCOM's core energy-management system lets users essentially shut off power in unsold rooms, while limiting usage in rooms that are rented but unoccupied.

"In a real crunch, we can take all the rented rooms that are occupied and actually let the temperature drift an extra two to three degrees," Buckingham said.

Such a strategy doesn't seriously affect guest comfort because peak demand periods might last only 12 to 18 minutes, after which settings return to normal, he said.

This approach—which INNCOM calls peak demand load shedding—can enable properties that already use energy efficiently to slash power-company premiums for heavy usage periods.

Conversely, Smart Systems International uses variable-rate banding to achieve results. At issue is how long it takes for a room's temperature to return to a guest's desired level once the guest returns.

"That's been the No. 1 issue that's prevented these systems from being adopted," said Thomas W. Kearin, SSI's chief financial officer.

To solve this glitch, the company employs an algorithm based on the thermodynamics of a room to guarantee an eight-minute recovery time with its systems.

Most guestroom energy-management systems allow temperatures to drift a fixed number of degrees from the guest's desired setting. But SSI's algorithms take into account factors such as outdoor temperatures and humidity levels and allow guestroom temperatures to drift no further from desired settings than the system can recover from in eight minutes or less.

All hoteliers are interested in a reasonable payback period—two years on average, although it can be substantially shorter depending on the level of one's utility rates—for energy-system investments.

They're also seeking upgrades to basic energy-management capabilities, according to Senercomm's Gomez.

In this area, capabilities offered by major vendors build upon basic occupancy sensing by adding links to a variety of devices and systems. Users of INNCOM's products, for example, can connect to a system of plates that allow housekeepers to receive "do not disturb" or "please make up room" messages on light-emitting diodes outside the rooms.

Interfaces to in-room refreshment systems likewise can eliminate the need for staffers to visually inspect minibars. Similar links to locking systems generate alarms if a guest inadvertently has left a patio or other door ajar.

Senercomm's system lets operators monitor the efficiency of in-room fan coils and generate alarms when problems are suspected.

"What we're doing is becoming a watchdog over the efficiency of heating and air-conditioning units," Gomez said. "It becomes a guest-satisfaction issue. We're automatically cutting a work order and sending a technician in before there's a guest complaint. One of the things that's surprising to a lot of hotel owners is the level of technology and how far it's gone. They're amazed when I show them what can be done."

Nevertheless, not everyone is convinced extended capabilities are worthwhile investments.

"Hoteliers are looking for simple solutions to existing problems regarding energy management, not something complex that's going to require a lot of extra work or maintenance for their staff," said William Fizer, president and c.e.o. of Lodging Technology Corp., which markets the Guestroom Energy Management System.

Rather than focusing on simple solutions that customers really want, he said some companies add bells and whistles to help sell products that sometimes cause more problems than they solve.

Future Functionality

Asked when the current round of energy-price hikes might cease, experts offered varying opinions.

"There will be ups and downs," Buckingham said. "Generally speaking, I think a higher plateau of energy costs has been established."

Anticipating further pressures, INNCOM is partnering with six organizations to introduce later this year a shared Ethernet platform that Buckingham said will pay for itself in savings while providing a backbone for services such as video on demand and high-speed Internet access.

"In the guestroom, I don't think you can save more energy then we're saving now without adversely impacting guest comfort," Buckingham said. "But you can improve the economic viability of installations by doing things like this shared Ethernet platform concept."

Through links with front-desk systems, this technology might automatically adjust lights and drapes before a guest reaches his or her room, Buckingham said.

Likewise, Senercomm plans to introduce wireless in-room communications capabilities by the end of the year. Gomez said that with the number of cellular and other devices available to guests, maintaining wireless communications will be a challenge.

"Looking five years out, we don't want to come up with a solution today that will eventually have protocol collision problems with the thousands of other devices that will be used in hotels," Gomez said. "Preventing such problems is one more way vendors can help hoteliers manage both their energy usage and guest-satisfaction levels."

Sometimes in science, an invention comes before a study tool. In the mid-twentieth century, researchers created doped semiconductor materials that controlled heat conductivity at a level never before seen. The trick since then has become how to study the heat transfer for a specific, defined area, which is the known unit's heat flux. In other words, scientists need to be able to measure what is going on within a material at the atomic level. If materials are to be designed atom by atom, then analysis of this structure is essential to know what improves or impedes the movement of heat.

Here, author Adam Barnes describes what properties a heat flux sensor should possess. In doing so, he provides a good overview of basic thermodynamic terms and principles. The definition section at the beginning of the paper is useful as a condensed reference source.

Since the publication of this paper, researchers have taken some of Barnes's ideas and put them and others into actual practice. In

early 2004, a team of researchers created a heat flux sensor that consisted, in part, of a laser beam microscope placed within an air vacuum chamber. It has helped researchers to analyze, and even to develop, better heat conducting and insulating materials. —JV

"Improving Accuracy in Heat Flux Measurements"
by Adam Barnes
Process Heating, November 2001

Perhaps because heat flux is an invisible quantity, many people have difficulty in making heat flux measurements in a way that will yield correct results. Although heat flux data can be very useful, a heat flux sensor must be carefully applied to insure correct measurements. The goal of this paper is to illuminate some of the important details of heat flux measurements so that common pitfalls can be avoided.

First Some Definitions

Heat flux is often confused with temperature, and although they are related, heat flux is often more useful. As in any technical discussion, keeping the terminology straight is important. Refer to this glossary if things start to get confusing.

- *Heat* is the movement of energy across a thermodynamic barrier, and is measured in Joules (J).

- *Heat transfer* is the rate at which energy moves across the thermodynamic barrier, measured in Watts (W), that is, Joules per second. Heat transfer occurs in three different modes, conduction, convection, and radiation.

- *Heat flux* is the rate of energy transfer per unit area, expressed in W/m^2 or W/cm^2. We will examine this in more detail below.

- *Temperature* is an indication of the amount of thermal energy present in a substance. Any temperature scale (Celsius, Fahrenheit, etc.) may be used as long as the units are kept consistent.

- *Conduction* is a mode of heat transfer through a substance, either solid or fluid, on a molecular level as a result of a temperature gradient being present.

- *Convection* is a mode of heat transfer when there is fluid flow. As in conduction, a temperature gradient must be present, but convection is influenced by fluid flow, which alters the temperature gradient.

- *Radiation* is a mode of heat transfer that occurs via electromagnetic radiation, and does not require any transport medium or material.

- A *thermocouple* is used to measure temperature. It consists of a junction between two different metals that will produce a voltage

proportional to the temperature difference between the endpoints of the wires due to the Seebeck effect. For a thermocouple to give an accurate reading, there must be a reference temperature at some point along the wires; that is, a point where the temperature for both thermocouple leads are the same. Frequently this is taken to be room temperature where the leads are connected to a voltmeter or electronic thermometer. For more accurate measurements, both leads are lowered to a known temperature, such as the ice point.

• A *thermopile* is essentially an array of thermocouples. By linking many thermocouples in series, the temperature sensitivity is increased. Like a thermocouple, the thermopile reads the temperature difference between two points. For a heat flux sensor, these two points are the top and bottom layers of the thermopile.

Heat Flux Sensor Construction

Understanding how heat flux sensors work can help a great deal in understanding how to use them. A heat flux sensor typically consists of a thermopile, or sometimes just a pair of thermocouples, in which the elements are separated by a thin layer of thermal resistance material. Under a temperature gradient, the two thermopile junction layers will be at different temperatures and so will register a voltage. The heat flux is proportional to this differential voltage. Notice that a temperature gradient must exist, otherwise both thermocouple junction layers will be at the same temperature and hence register no voltage. The thermal resistance layer is usually as thin as possible to improve the response time of the sensor. To help insure a proper thermal gradient, heat flux sensors should be designed to have a high thermal conductivity.

Radiation Measurements and the Importance of Emissivity

All heat flux transducers made by Vatell are calibrated using radiative heat sources, because they are the most consistently repeatable. However, the fraction of the radiation absorbed by the transducer is never 100 %, and so the *absorbed* heat flux differs from the *incident* heat flux. The relation of incident and absorbed heat flux for a radiation source is given by

$$q''_{ab} = \varepsilon q''_{in} \qquad (1)$$

where

ε is the emissivity

All Vatell heat flux transducers are calibrated in terms of incident heat flux, so that for a radiative heat flux measurement, the heat flux is simply the output voltage divided by the sensitivity of the transducer. One should note that the emissivity is a function of wavelength, and so can change for radiative heat sources with different spectrums. Vatell transducers are typically coated with a high temperature black paint, which has an emissivity of 0.94 and a fairly flat spectral response over most wavelengths of interest. The output voltage from the transducer is a function of the heat flux and the sensitivity, which can be expressed as:

$$V_o = S_{in} q''_{in} = S_{ab} q''_{ab} \qquad (2)$$

where

V_o is the output voltage of the transducer

S_{in} is the sensitivity of the transducer for incident radiative heat flux; this number is given on the calibration certificate

q''_{in} is the incident heat flux

S_{ab} is the sensitivity of the transducer for absorbed heat flux

q''_{ab} is the absorbed heat flux

The sensitivity to incident and absorbed heat flux is related by the emissivity as:

$$S_{in} = \varepsilon\, S_{ab} \qquad (3)$$

To find the incident heat flux from a radiation source, use the equation

$$q''_{in} = \frac{V_o}{S_{in}} \qquad (4)$$

If the standard coating is removed or replaced with some other coating of known emissivity, the new emissivity must be used to calculate incident heat flux. For example, if the transducer is coated with colloidal graphite that has an emissivity of 0.82, the radiative heat flux would be given by

$$q''_{in} = \frac{V_o}{S_{in}} \cdot \frac{\epsilon_{Standard}}{\epsilon_{graphite}} \tag{5}$$

Conduction Measurements

When the heat flux is not from a radiation source, the sensitivity should be scaled by the emissivity because the emissivity only affects radiation measurements. For a conductive heat flux, the governing equation is

$$q''_{ab} = -k\frac{\delta T}{\delta n} = \frac{V_o}{S_{ab}} = \frac{V_o\epsilon}{S_{in}} \tag{6}$$

where

k is the thermal conductance

$\frac{\delta T}{\delta n}$ is the thermal gradient with n as the unit vector normal to the surface across which the heat flux is being measured.

Convection Measurements

As with conduction measurements, when measuring convective heat flux the sensitivity must be scaled by the emissivity to determine the proper value. For convection, the heat flux equation is

$$q''_{ab} = h\Delta T = \frac{V_o}{S_{ab}} = \frac{V_o\epsilon}{S_{in}} \tag{7}$$

where

> h is the heat transfer coefficient.
>
> ΔT is the temperature difference between the transducer and the fluid.

The heat transfer coefficient is a function of the thermal conductivity of the fluid, and the fluid flow characteristics. Unfortunately fluid flow is extremely complex and difficult to model; consequently the heat transfer coefficient is difficult to determine except in an empirical fashion. Heat flux transducers are commonly used in fact to determine the heat transfer coefficient. By using the heat flux measurement in conjunction with temperature measurements of the fluid and the transducer face to obtain a ΔT, the heat transfer coefficient can be found. This procedure assumes that the heat transfer coefficient for the transducer and the surrounding system are the same, so that the incident and absorbed heat fluxes are equal. The accuracy of this assumption will vary with different system configurations and materials. In general, the less the transducer alters the system the better.

Measurements with Mixed Modes of Heat Transfer

All three modes of heat transfer can be measured as described above. Conductive and convective modes can be mixed without any loss of accuracy in the measurement, assuming the incident and absorbed convective heat fluxes are equal. When radiation is mixed with the other modes however, there is the question of what fraction of the heat flux needs to be corrected for emissivity, and what fraction does not. Ideally the different modes can be isolated so that the question does not occur; for example, using a radiometer to view only radiation sources. If the modes cannot be differentiated experimentally, some intelligent estimates of the relative fractions of the heat flux that each mode contributes must be made. In these cases the emissivity of the heat flux sensor should be as high as possible to minimize error. Some sensors are restricted to the mode of heat transfer for which they can be used, *e.g.* a Gardon gauge should only be used for detection of radiation. Other sensors, such as the Vatell HFM or Episensor, can measure heat transfer in any mode.

Mounting Considerations

Now that the operation of the heat flux sensor is understood, some potential mounting difficulties can be examined. The presence of a heat flux sensor will invariably alter the heat flux distribution where it is mounted. The idea is to minimize this disruption as much as possible while still achieving good sensor output. The exact mounting will depend on the system geometry, materials, and modes of heat transfer.

Heat flux sensors have two basic shapes, either a flat, surfaced-attached, layered wafer or a insert-style cylinder. The surface-attached configuration usually has a greater sensitivity than cylindrical designs because of greater surface area. However, cylindrical sensors generally can withstand higher temperatures, and can more easily be water-cooled.

The first issue to take into account is the thermal gradient across the sensor. If there is no thermal gradient, no heat flux will be measured. This is especially important in long duration tests in which a sensor may heat up to a uniform temperature. In these cases the sensor will probably need to be actively cooled. Because of the need for a thermal gradient, heat flux sensors do not function well if they are not mounted, because they will quickly come to a uniform or near-uniform temperature without some way to dissipate absorbed heat. This also means one must be careful mounting a heat flux sensor in a substrate with a high thermal conductivity like copper or aluminum. Such materials will have little or no thermal gradient because heat distributes itself so quickly. As a general guideline, the thermal conductivity of the sensor should be the same or larger than the material in which it is mounted for good heat flux measurements. For some sensors, like the Vatell HFM series, the thermal conductivity of the sensor is so high (equivalent conductivity to aluminum) that it will function in almost any substrate.

The next factor to consider is thermal contact resistance. If a heat flux sensor does not make good thermal contact with the material it is to be measuring, the sensor will cause a local hot spot to form (or a cold spot in the case where the heat flux is negative). This hot spot will alter thermal gradients and change the convective and conductive heat transfer coefficients. For this reason, cylindrical sensors are usually pressed into a substrate or held tightly into place with a mounting nut. Flat, layered sensors are usually mounted with a thermally conductive adhesive to minimize contact resistance. Simply butting a sensor against a surface may still result in a heat flux reading, but the contact resistance will keep the reading from being particularly meaningful. In a similar vein, water-cooling a sensor must be done carefully, because a temperature mismatch between the sensor and the substrate will occur, which may skew measurements.

Fluid flow, whether gas or liquid, must be examined as well. This convection can be forced (*e.g.* a jet of gas or liquid in a pipe) or natural (*e.g.* hot air rising). The heat flux sensor disturbs the convection in a system in two ways, physically and thermally. Physically the sensor creates a discontinuity in the surface, even if it is mounted flush. The more the sensor protrudes from the surface, the greater the disruption. Thermally, the sensor alters the local temperature gradient due to its physical protrusion. The impact of the disruption the sensor causes will depend on the speed of the fluid flow. The disruption is greater for a laminar flow than for a turbulent one because of the rapidly changing, chaotic nature of the latter. The system can be considered effectively undisturbed when [3]

$$\frac{\delta k_{sensor}}{R k_{substrate}} \ll 1 \tag{8}$$

where

δ is the thickness of the sensor.

k_{sensor} is the thermal conductivity of the sensor.

$k_{substrate}$ is the thermal conductivity of the substrate.

R is the radius of the sensor.

When dealing with a radiation source, two factors in particular must be considered. The first is the emissivity of the sensor, as discussed earlier. The second is the distance of the sensor from the source. Because heat flux drops with the square of the distance from the source, the sensor must be positioned carefully to insure accurate measurements. That is to say, if the surface of interest is 10 cm away from the radiation source, the sensor should take measurements 10 cm away from the source. If the radiation source does not emit in a spatially uniform pattern, the sensor position relative to the source becomes important. For example, a lit candle does not emit in a spatially uniform pattern because the heat flux is much higher directly over the flame than it is to the side.

Conclusions

The issues discussed above will hopefully serve as a useful guide in making heat flux measurements. However, a comprehensive look at the thermodynamics and fluid dynamics associated with heat flux measurement is beyond the scope of this paper. For more detailed information, the interested reader is encouraged to begin with the listed references.

References

1. Diller, T. E. "Advances in Heat Flux Measurements," *Advances in Heat Transfer Volume 23*, Academic Press, pp. 279–368, 1993.
2. Schmidt, F. W, and R. E. Henderson, C. H. Wolgemuth, "Introduction to Thermal Sciences—Thermodynamics, Fluid Dynamics, Heat Transfer," John Wiley & Sons, 1984.
3. Wesley, D. A. "Thin disk on a convectively cooled plate—application to heat flux measurement errors," ASME Journal of Heat Transfer, vol. 82, pp. 341–348, 1979.

Using Thermodynamics to Study Natural Networks

4

What does a hive full of bees have in common with a machine, the design of trees, and how oxygen circulates throughout our bodies? At first, this group would seem to have little in common, but this article suggests that fundamental principles of physics govern many, if not all, of the functions of these diverse systems. The basic idea lies in the fact that systems, whether man-made or natural, all have the same goal of optimizing operation. Controlling temperature and maintaining a good energy flow are two ways of doing this.

As author Adrian Bejan states, bees position themselves in their hives to adjust temperature. Tree cells grow in patterns to help with air, water, and nutrient uptake. The human body distributes oxygen in such a way that high-energy organs like the heart and lungs get enough oxygen without depleting the rest of the body.

The notion that a handful of rules governs everything is not relatively new, but the debate has heated up in recent years. Many prestigious

*journals and physics organizations have pub-
lished articles, such as this one, and held seminars
on subjects that seek to find equations and
formulas that might explain all systems. Perhaps
it is the next logical step from the condensation of
principles into the three laws of thermodynamics,
or Newton's laws, that generated excitement in
past centuries. —JV*

"How Nature Takes Shape"
by Adrian Bejan
Mechanical Engineering-CIME, October 1997

The principles used to design heat exchangers can now
be applied to predict the structure of trees and other
natural networks.

Although physicists and biologists have dominated
the debate over the origins and evolution of nature,
engineers may hold the key that will bridge the gaps
between these and other fields as well as answer such
fundamental questions with authority. After all, the
same principles that engineers use to design, construct,
and operate manmade systems apply to the animate and
inanimate structures that surround us. Both natural
and man-made systems have purpose and finite size,
they are often subject to flow and size constraints,
and—through natural or man-made processes—they
are optimized and constructed. As a result, engineers are
well equipped to account for the behavior of such
systems as they form and evolve in an identifiable
direction that can be aligned with time itself.

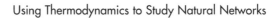

Thermodynamics represents a powerful tool that engineers can use to gain a more profound understanding of how naturally organized systems arise and evolve. Since the dramatic rise in the cost of fuel in the 1970s, engineers have applied thermodynamics to improve the performance, increase the efficiency, and lower the cost of man-made systems. In the process, engineers have extended the theory that underlies thermodynamics—which was originally conceived to define engine performance in terms of heat and work—so that it also applies to the operation and optimization of highly complex systems. Thermoeconomics and the analysis of exergy (the loss of available energy) are examples of such applications. Even more important, engineers have simultaneously applied the principles of thermodynamics, fluid mechanics, and heat and mass transfer to construct models that account for the inherent irreversibility of processes executed by a system—natural or man-made—and its components.

This development, known as entropy-generation minimization, is an aspect of thermodynamic optimization that sheds considerable light on the organization of the natural world. In the process of performing such analyses, engineers determine the entropy that a system generates as a function of its physical parameters, including size, shapes, and materials. After gaining this understanding, engineers—at least in theory—can go on to optimize the system's performance in terms of its constraints, which are responsible for its irreversible operation.

For example, engineers can use the energy-minimization method to optimize the "rhythm" of intermittent processes in which irreversibility is caused by time-dependent diffusion—the growth of a layer of ice on a cooled surface, for instance. Thickness of the ice increases with the square root of the duration of the freezing process. The rate of ice production decreases, however, as the freezing process continues. If the purpose of the system is to maximize the production of ice (or refrigeration or exergy storage), engineers can "optimize" the freezing process by periodically interrupting it, scraping the surface clean, and restarting the process. The time-averaged rate of ice production is proportional to the square root of the duration of freezing divided by the freezing and surface-cleaning times. Using this knowledge, engineers can maximize ice production by fine-tuning the on-and-off freezing process.

Such rhythms can help engineers understand a wide variety of man-made and natural phenomena. For example, engineers could proceed in this way to predict the existence of unique, finely tuned frequencies for heartbeats and breathing, which decrease as body size increases. Such allometric laws, which have been observed empirically in biology for quite some time, can now be anticipated theoretically according to engineering thermodynamics and entropy-generation minimization.

Of course, the larger issue here is not just to observe and describe such processes but also to understand the purpose of the optimization that rules a naturally occurring structure. After all, when engineers design a

device or system, they must first understand its purpose. The device must function—fulfill its purpose—subject to certain constraints. Merely analyzing the device is not sufficient; the real objective is to optimize it, construct it, and make it work. The unique understanding that engineers offer in the search for the origins and evolution of naturally occurring structures is that many "designs" for such structures—just like those for manmade ones have nearly the same overall performance as the optimal design, even though they differ in their finer details.

Put another way, this engineering insight helps account for the evolution of naturally occurring systems—at least those subject to flow and size constraints—from the simple to the complex. Understanding how nature is "engineered"—in other words, grasping the thermodynamic principles underlying a naturally occurring structure's finite size, constraints, optimization, and construction can help engineers determine how a shape occurs and how a structure develops as it moves from one scale to the next larger scale.

Perhaps the best way to illustrate this concept is to consider the topology of a structure and the way its components interact. Using thermodynamic-optimization methods, engineers can determine the optimal dimensions of components. For example, in the most elementary passage of a heat exchanger, the generation of entropy is due to both heat transfer and fluid friction, which compete against one another. The hydraulic diameter of the passage can be selected such that the sum of the two irreversibilities is minimal. The dimensions of bodies immersed in external convection can be selected in a similar way. Even simpler is the sizing of a system in which a single transport mechanism causes the irreversibility, such as heat transfer. When the heat current is imposed, minimizing the entropy generation means minimizing the resistance to heat flow.

To cool electronic packages, for example, both the volume and the heat-generation rate that is distributed uniformly over that volume are fixed. The heat current is removed by a single-phase stream with natural or forced convection. The geometric arrangement of heat-generating components can then be optimized such that the hot-spot temperature is minimal. In attempting such an arrangement, the plate-to-plate spacing (or number of columns) is free to vary. If the spacing is too large, however, there is not enough heat-transfer area and the hot-spot temperature becomes high; when the spacing is too small, the coolant flow rate decreases and the hot-spot temperature is again high. Between the two lies an optimal spacing—an optimal package architecture—that minimizes the thermal resistance between the system and the environment. This geometric principle is applied in many man-made and natural systems. A swarm of bees, for example, regulates its maximum internal temperature by constructing similar cooling channels; the bees rearrange themselves to create vertical (internal-chimney) channels through the swarm.

Researchers recently discovered that, when minimizing the thermal resistance between a fixed heat-generating volume and one point, every portion—

every subsystem of the given volume—can have its shape optimized. This principle can be illustrated at the smallest volume scale, where a single high-conductivity fiber removes the heat generated by the low-conductivity material from the system. Ultimately, an optimal rectangular shape can be found to minimize the thermal resistance between the element and the exit end of its high-conductivity fiber.

The same geometric-optimization principle applies at larger scales. The next volume is an assembly of optimized volume elements of the smallest size. This construct can also have its shape (or number of constituents) optimized. The process of construction and shape optimization continues toward stepwise larger scales until the given volume is covered. The end result is shape and structure—the optimized architecture of the composite (high- and low-conductivity materials) that connects the sink point to the finite-size volume. The high-conductivity paths form a tree, and the low-conductivity paths reach the infinity of points of the given volume.

Tree networks abound in nature, in both animate and inanimate flow systems. We find them everywhere: plants, leaves, roots, lungs, vascular tissues, neural dendrites, river drainage basins, lightning, and dendritic crystals. Every detail of every natural tree, for example, can be anticipated through the construction and optimization shown for the heat tree already discussed. In fluid trees, the small-scale volumetric flow is by slow viscous diffusion (such as Darcy flow in the wet banks of the smallest rivulet), while the larger scale flow is

organized into faster conduits. The high-conductivity channels form a tree. More important, each feature of the tree is deterministic, the result of a single principle of optimization.

This conclusion runs counter to currently accepted doctrine that natural structures are nondeterministic, the result of chance and necessity. In fractal geometry, any tree can be simulated by repeating an assumed algorithm and truncating this operation at an arbitrary, small (finite) scale. But fractal geometry is descriptive, not predictive. The discovery, then, is the mechanism that generates this structure, from one scale to the next.

Shape and Structure in Nature

Volume-to-point constructs have a definite time direction: from small to large, and from shapelessness (diffusion) to structure (channels and streams). Determinism results only if this time arrow is respected. If the time direction is reversed, such as from large to small, through the repeated fracturing of a postulated network into smaller and smaller pieces (as in fractal geometry), then it is impossible to predict the optimal volume-to-point flow architecture.

The optimized geometry formed by low- and high-conductivity flow regimes unites all the volume-to-point flows. Think of how oxygen flows through a mammal: The low-conductivity flow is volumetric mass diffusion through tissues, while the high-conductivity flow is stream flow through blood vessels and bronchial passages. Also consider turbulent flow: Diffusion in the smallest volume elements is accompanied by the structure of faster currents known as eddies. Artificial constructs, such as the internal arrangement of components in a computer, require the same cooperation between slow and fast heat transfer, with the slow mode placed at the smallest scale.

This pattern of cooperation is also responsible for the formation of societal trees, from bacterial colonies to urban growth. Every member of the living group has a place in the structure, in such a way that every member benefits. The urge to organize is thus an expression of selfish behavior, i.e., actions for the good of the individual rather than of the group.

The geometric principle that generates tree networks in living groups is even clearer in the context of minimizing the travel time between one point and a finite-size area with an infinity of points. Travelers in this hypothetical area have access to more than one mode of locomotion, starting with the slowest speed (walking) and proceeding toward faster modes. The given area is covered in steps of increasingly larger constructs. Each construct can be optimized for overall shape and angle between assembly and constituents.

This theory predicts urban growth, from backyards and alleys to streets, avenues, and highways. Along the way, we discover that tree networks are results of a unique geometric optimization principle. The principle represents the physics behind fractals, the reason why natural tree networks happen to look like the truncated fractal images postulated by mathematicians.

In the past, the minimization of travel time has been invoked to account for the shape of light rays. Research as far back as Heron of Alexandria has shown that when the ray strikes a mirror, the optimal angle of incidence equals the angle of reflection. We were also taught that the ray is bent to an optimal angle as it passes from one medium into another.

This travel time, or the principle of minimizing resistance, suggests a generalization: For a finite-size system to persist in time—that is, to live—it must evolve in such a way that it provides easier access to the imposed currents that flow through it. This statement recognizes the natural tendency of imposed currents to construct paths of optimal access (such as shapes and structures) through constrained open systems. It also accounts for the evolution (improvement) of these paths, which occurs in an identifiable direction that can be aligned with time.

This generalization accounts for the "choices" that are made by natural and man-made macroscopic open systems subject to flow and size constraints. It bridges the gaps not only between physics, biology, economics, and many related fields but also between physics and engineering. Moreover, it introduces engineering insights into the current debate on natural order—and rightfully so. Nature is the supreme form of engineering design and organization. Who is better qualified than an engineer to extend the deterministic powers of thermodynamics so that they help account for the grand design of the natural world?

Article courtesy of *Mechanical Engineering* magazine Vol. 119/No. 9, September, 1997, pages 90–92; copyright *Mechanical Engineering* magazine (the American Society of Mechanical Engineers International).

A mind-blowing realization about many physics principles is that several can apply to any closed system. What then is a closed system? A machine, such as a computer, easily falls into that category, but what about human beings, Earth, and the entire universe? Each is a system in and of its own right.

This article takes such an expanded viewpoint by discussing how the second law of thermodynamics, which concerns entropy, might apply to Earth's climate. Specifically, it addresses maximum entropy production, or MEP. Heat is energy, and therefore it can produce work. A pot over a hot stove surface can boil water contained in the pot. The boiling is work.

Similarly, when heat from the Sun beams down on Earth, gases in the atmosphere and water react and can produce work in the way of wind, rain, and other weather events. Since work does not seem to make full use of the Sun's energy, some of the energy is displaced in a disorderly fashion. This measure of disorder is entropy. When the atmosphere is in a state of maximum work output, it is also in MEP.

Physicists can calculate entropy, but that assumes the data input into the equations is correct. Given that humans have affected Earth's atmosphere by introducing pollutants into it, the data likely is not correct for any given moment. That is one of many reasons why climate modeling remains an incorrect science, at least for now. It helps to explain why your local weatherman may predict rain on a day that turns out to be sunny and mild. —JV

"Full Steam Ahead—Probably"
by Ralph Lorenz
Science, **February 7, 2003**

Complex systems like Earth's climate may organize themselves to produce entropy at the maximum rate permitted by their circumstance. A paper in the *Journal of Physics A* (1) shows why, but concedes that it is only usually true.

Carnot (2) compared the flow of heat from hot to cold to the downhill flow of water, although he said nothing about how fast the heat would flow. Much modern thermodynamics considers just such non-equilibrium situations in which an external input flow of energy keeps things moving. Planetary climate is just such a situation, with the tropics being kept warm by extra sunlight. As heat flows from warm to cold, it can perform work, generating our weather. But how much work?

Edward Lorenz (3), the "father of chaos," pointed out in 1960 that the work output of Earth's atmosphere might be close to the maximum possible. Based on the observed state of the Earth, he argued that if the heat flow were lower than it is, the resulting large temperature gradients would drive motions more vigorously. The system should therefore tend to a maximum in work output.

More recent investigations tend to be inspired by the work of Paltridge (4). Likening the ever-increasing resolution of general circulation models (GCMs) to attempts to understand a gas by monitoring every molecule, Paltridge sought an overall principle that might capture the net behavior of the atmosphere. He found that satisfactory agreement with Earth's climate state could be obtained by assuming that the atmospheric heat transports organized themselves to a maximum entropy production (MEP) state—a state in which the work output, the product of the heat flux and the temperature gradient driving it, is largest.

Like the Gaia hypothesis, this idea smacks of endowing the system with teleological intent and presents philosophical challenges to the deterministic dynamical approach of conventional meteorology. It suffered from two main criticisms. First, Paltridge's result, while not disputed, could simply be coincidence. But that argument became harder to sustain with the realization (5) that Saturn's moon Titan seems also to be in an MEP state: The temperatures observed there require heat transport to be very weak, as predicted from MEP, whereas the conventional expectation would be that transport should be very strong on this small, slowly rotating world with its thick atmosphere.

A second objection was that Paltridge offered no reason for why systems should choose this state. Dewar's paper (1) may have finally filled that void by showing, with the formal algebra of information theory and statistical mechanics developed by Jaynes (6), how the maximum entropy production state becomes the most probable state—if the system is forced weakly enough to be able to choose which state to reside in.

This result is not an imperative, but rather a statistical likelihood. This lack of rigor applies to the second law of thermodynamics itself. The second law says entropy must increase. Yet, the statistics of atomic collisions are such that every so often more molecules will hit an object (such as a pollen grain) on one side than on the other, and the object will appear to move spontaneously—an apparent gain of ordered kinetic energy from nowhere. Energy is conserved, in that the molecules transfer it to the object, but entropy fleetingly decreases, in that the random motions of molecules have conspired to move a macroscopic object. The statistics of these fluctuations, whose probability tends to zero as the duration or magnitude rises, were recently determined (7) in a delicate experiment to be exactly in accordance with predictions.

We can also use a statistical approach to determine whether Earth's climate is in an MEP state. There are many modes of transporting heat. Some, like fluctuating winds, involve lots of mechanical dissipation (8), whereas others, like the ocean currents, do not (see the figure [in the original article]). A steady-state solution will balance the dissipation required by the combination of modes with the work that the corresponding heat flow can produce. Despite the empirical agreement tuned into GCMs, this is an underconstrained problem with many possible solutions. Similar problems are encountered in astronomy when trying to determine which of many possible original images was blurred by an imperfect telescope to yield the observed smudge.

A "best guess" approach to such underconstrained problems was advocated by Jaynes, whose work is extended by Dewar. The best guess is that which has the highest Shannon entropy (a measure of information content). As long as the system can choose from a rich ensemble of modes, it follows that it will most probably reside in or close to the states with maximum dissipation. These states offer the largest number of possible solutions (combinations of modes that exactly dissipate the work that is produced). Similar ideas have been explored in river network self-organization (9).

The MEP idea also holds for constrained nonequilibrium systems that fix the gradient or flux—such as the temperature gradient in a Rayleigh-Benard convection experiment (in which a fluid is heated from below), or the sand flux on a sandpile (10). In response to the constraint, the systems maximize the other parameter—the heat flow in convection, the angle in the sandpile experiment—thereby maximizing their product, the entropy production. As a result, the heat flux in convection is maximized, and the angle of a sandpile is generally limited to the angle of repose.

Dewar's work puts MEP on a much sounder footing. Laboratory investigations that demonstrate MEP would be an important further advance. The growth of N_HCl crystals has already been shown (11) to switch modes to select MEP. Entropy production is now being explored in numerical climate models. In one recent study (12), perturbations to an ocean circulation model always resulted in a jump to a state with higher entropy production, except when the perturbation destroyed the system's initial state altogether.

Some puzzles remain. All else being equal, MEP would predict a planet's meridional temperature contrast to be independent of its rotation rate. This disagrees with some rudimentary GCM experiments, and with meteorologists' intuition. The MEP idea continues to generate considerable friction among climate modelers—but perhaps that is exactly what we should expect.

References

(1.) R. L. Dewar, *J. Phys. A. Math. Gen.* 36, 631 (2003); (preprint available at http://arxiv.org/abs/condmat/0005382).

(2.) S. Carnot, *Reflections on the Motive Power of Heat* (Bachelier, Paris, 1824).

(3.) E. N. Lorenz, in *Dynamics of Climate*, R. L. Pfeifer, Ed. (Pergamon, Oxford, 1960), pp. 86–92.

(4.) G. W. Paltridge, *Q. J. R. Meteorol. Soc.* 101, 475 (1975).

(5.) R. D. Lorenz, J. I. Lunine, C. P. McKay, P. G. Withers, *Geophys. Res. Lett.* 28, 415 (2001).

(6.) E. T. Jaynes, *Phys. Rev.* 106, 620 (1957).

(7.) G. M. Wang, E. M. Sevick, E. Mittag, D. J. Searles, D. J. Evans, *Phys. Rev. Lett.* 89, 050601 (2002).

(8.) R. D. Lorenz, *J. Non-Equilib. Thermodyn.* 27, 229 (2002).

(9.) A. Rinaldo et al., *Phys. Rev. Lett.* 76, 3364 (1996).

(10.) P. Bak, *How Nature Works* (Springer-Verlag, New York, 1998).

(11.) A. Hill, *Nature* 148, 426 (1990).

(12.) S. Shimokawa, H. Ozawa, *Q. J. R. Meteorol. Soc.* 128, 2115 (2002).

The basic components of our environment, water and air, hardly seem like the stuff of great mystery, but they are. Just recently, scientists determined that air in the atmosphere is heavier than previously thought. Here, NASA scientists reveal that water freezes differently than most

experts suspected before this research was conducted.

The discovery that water freezes first at its surface and not in the middle of a droplet may seem like a good bit of trivia but of little other consequence. Keep in mind that water has a profound effect on climate. Every year, weather threats, such as hurricanes, result in human deaths and property damage. One reason is that climatologists still cannot predict weather with 100 percent accuracy. That is because no one fully understands the dynamics of weather basics, such as how temperature affects water and how water turns from a liquid into a crystalline structure, ice. As writer S. Perkins mentions, related studies on water will allow for better computer modeling. That, in turn, should lead to more accurate weather reports in the future. —JV

"Clearing Up How Cloud Droplets Freeze—Outside-In"
by S. Perkins
Science News, November 30, 2002

A fresh look at old experimental data is threatening to overturn a longstanding theory about how water droplets freeze within clouds.

Suspended water droplets can remain liquid even when they and the air that surrounds them have temperatures far below the normal freezing point, says Azadeh Tabazadeh, an atmospheric chemist at NASA's

Ames Research Center in Mountain View, Calif. Data collected in recent years show that clouds as cold as $-37.5°C$ can still contain many supercooled droplets. Such droplets freeze solid almost instantly if they bump into each other or are otherwise disturbed.

Familiar as clouds are, the behavior of their constituent droplets remains only partly understood. This conceptual fog is particularly thick for conditions in which there aren't many particles in the air, says Tabazadeh.

Most scientists have long assumed that a tiny globule of pure, supercooled water, when disturbed, begins to freeze around an icy seed that suddenly forms inside it. According to this scenario, the time needed to freeze a given volume of water—say, 1 liter dispersed into a fine mist—is independent of the size of the individual droplets because the formation of a seed particle is a chance event.

But the results of recent laboratory experiments, when combined with information garnered from tests conducted as many as 30 years ago, don't back up that scenario. Together, the data indicate that the time needed to freeze a given volume of supercooled water varies drastically—by a factor of up to 100,000—according to droplet size, says Tabazadeh. She and her colleagues report their analysis in an upcoming *Proceedings of the National Academy of Sciences*.

This extreme variation makes sense if freezing begins at the surface of the drops, not at the cores. Dividing a given volume of water into a large number of small droplets yields more total surface area than if the volume is split into a small number of large drops,

Tabazadeh explains. The freezing rate would then depend on the surface area.

The laws of thermodynamics also argue against ice nuclei forming inside supercooled droplets, says Howard Reiss, a physical chemist at the University of California, Los Angeles and a coauthor of the new report.

When water molecules begin to assemble into ice crystals, they release large amounts of latent heat. If that process occurred in the center of a supercooled droplet, the heat would remain trapped within the globule, slowing the freezing process. But if crystallization begins at the droplet's surface, latent heat can more easily transfer to the surrounding air. In this case, the droplets are so cold that heat released internally as the crystallization proceeds probably wouldn't melt the developing ice, says Tabazadeh.

Lightning, rainfall, and other meteorological phenomena vary with the ratio of water droplets and ice particles in clouds, says Lawrence Hipps, a meteorologist at Utah State University in Logan. Linking freezing rates of clouds to those atmospheric and other climate processes is one of the most unreliable areas in current climate simulations, Hipps adds. "It's important to understand how clouds operate if we ever expect to model them," he says.

Common sense tells us that a solid is denser than a liquid. If a worker spilled liquid cement

on his foot, he would not feel much pain. However, if the same amount fell down as a hardened solid, it is likely that he would remember the event because the material was denser.

Scientists often study solid-liquid phase changes, as well as liquid-gas changes. Usually a solid is denser. Water, however, is a notable exception. When water freezes and becomes ice, the ice is less dense than the water. That is why ice floats in your water, soda, iced tea, or other liquid beverage.

On a microscopic level, the hydrogen within water changes structure to create a crystalline form, which is ice. This would seem to be basic science, but experts are still puzzled by what goes on at the atomic level. Since ice is less dense than water, it makes sense that water gains density as it gets colder. Surprisingly, there is a point where this process stops and leads to the crystallization. In addition, water's measure of diffusion also decreases at an unexpected rate. Writer Alan Soper discusses these puzzling phenomena in this article. —JV

"Water and Ice"
by Alan K. Soper
Science, August 23, 2002

To the nonspecialist, it must come as a bit of a surprise to discover how much scientific attention is paid to the apparently simple water molecule, H_2O. Almost every week, new results on water and ice appear in high-profile journals, while lesser molecules like hydrogen fluoride or ammonia seem to get little or no coverage.

The apparent simplicity of the water molecule belies the enormous complexity of its interactions with other molecules, including other water molecules. In common with all other molecules, it experiences repulsive overlap and attractive van der Waals forces, but added to this is the strongly directional force of hydrogen bonding. A satisfactory description of this force still eludes scientists. In water, the strength and directionality of the hydrogen bond combine with molecular geometry in a way that sets this molecule apart from almost any other, giving water its complex and still poorly understood phase diagram (see the figure [in the original article]).

A well-known aspect of this phase diagram is the fact that at ambient pressure and 0°C (273 K), ice is less dense than water, and that the liquid is less dense at 0°C than at +4°C. In fact, if you supercool the liquid below 0°C at ambient pressure, it continues to become less dense (1). But this process does not continue indefinitely. At about −40°C (233 K), the liquid will spontaneously crystallize, no matter how pure it is (2). This temperature, known as the homogeneous nucleation temperature (HNT), is the cause of much controversy that remains unresolved.

But the plot gets even thicker. As water is supercooled, its diffusion constant diminishes, and appears by extrapolation to go to zero just below the HNT. This observation has led to the conjecture that there is a "stability limit" to the supercooled liquid (3). For water, however, this limit is not the usual glass transition temperature, as it would be for many other liquids. Instead, it represents the start of a region where disordered water apparently cannot exist. The glass transition temperature for water is in fact much lower, probably around 136 K.

One simple method of circumventing this "no man's land" in the water phase diagram is to take hexagonal ice at 77 K and pressurize it to about 2 GPa (4). This process leads to a dense form of amorphous ice, called high-density amorphous ice (HDA), which remains dense if kept below $\sim$ 100 K. But if HDA is warmed to $\sim$ 115 K, it suddenly expands to another form of amorphous ice called low-density amorphous ice (LDA). LDA appears to be similar in structure to the amorphous ice produced by vapor deposition and hyperquenching of the liquid.

The suddenness of the HDA-LDA transition was one of several factors leading to the conjecture that water exhibits a liquid-liquid critical point below which two different forms of liquid water coexist (5). This tantalizing suggestion, which was based on a computer simulation, went a long way toward explaining, at least qualitatively, many of the anomalous properties of water. It was, however, controversial, because the proposed location of the second critical point at 200 K was in the middle of the region where, according to the stability limit conjecture, bulk water can only exist in crystalline form.

If there really is a liquid-liquid critical point in water, then the transition from one liquid to the other must be first-order, that is, discontinuous in density. If LDA and HDA are the low-temperature manifestations of these two forms of water, then the transition from LDA to HDA or vice versa, must be sudden. But is the HDA-LDA transition really sudden, or does the structure relax in a stepwise fashion via a series of intermediate structures? Could the relaxation even be continuous? Tulk et al. (6) provide experimental evidence for such a continuum. (Of course, if HDA and LDA are not the low-temperature forms of the two purported liquids, then there might be some new forms of water out there still to be discovered.)

Another known liquid water phase may provide some clues to the low-temperature behavior of water. In the stable liquid phase just above the melting point, the structure of water undergoes a characteristic and continuous transition from an open network structure at low pressures to a much denser form at high pressure. As the density increases, the tetrahedral arrangement of nearest-neighbor molecules found in ordinary water and hexagonal ice is preserved, as it is in many of the phases of ice. However, beyond the nearest-neighbor tetrahedron, the hydrogen bonds become increasingly bent or broken as the pressure (and hence density) is increased.

At the temperature at which HDA is stable, the transition from LDA to HDA cannot be induced directly, because the material is invariably in powdered form and hence the density cannot be increased continuously by applying hydrostatic pressure. Instead, Tulk et al. attempt to capture amorphous ice in its intermediate states by carefully annealing samples of HDA at different temperatures. After each annealing, they cool the samples to 40 K and measure their x-ray and neutron diffraction patterns. The results seem unambiguous: A whole series of intermediate (and possibly continuous) structures is found, and the diffraction patterns cannot be represented as a linear combination of the diffraction patterns of HDA and LDA.

In other words, the intermediate structures must be distinct from those of both of these amorphous ices. If this interpretation is correct, then HDA and LDA cannot exist as unique entities. Tulk et al.'s evidence for a continuous, or quasi-continuous, transition between LDA and HDA (6) makes it more difficult to support a thesis that there is some point in the water phase diagram where two distinct disordered forms of water can coexist.

Of course, one experiment does not resolve all the issues. The liquid-liquid critical point scenario has spawned many theoretical and experimental studies, and it does provide one of the first qualitative frameworks for describing water properties. Nonetheless, alternative scenarios such as that described in (7) can also be quite successful at predicting water properties. What is certain is that experiments like that reported by Tulk et al. (6) will provoke ever more incisive techniques for looking at water at the molecular level.

References

(1.) G. S. Kell, *J. Chem. Eng. Data* 20, 97 (1975).

(2.) R. J. Speedy, *J. Phys. Chem.* 86, 982 (1982).

(3.) F. X. Prielmeier, E. W. Lang, R. J. Speedy, H.-D. Ludemann, *Phys. Rev. Lett.* 59, 1128 (1987).

(4.) O. Mishima et al., *Nature* 310, 393 (1984).

(5.) P. H. Poole, F. Sciortino, U. Essmann, H. E. Stanley, *Nature* 360, 324 (1992).

(6.) C. A. Tulk et al., *Science* 297, 1320 (2002).

(7.) T. M. Truskett, P. G. Debenedetti, S. Sastry, S. Torquato, *J. Chem. Phys.* 111, 2647 (1999).

5 Thermodynamics of Human and Plant Cells

Electricity is measured in volts, and we are all familiar with the volt measurements posted on appliances, adaptors, and similar equipment. What may be more of a surprise is that a single human body cell, such as a cell on your tongue, also experiences measurable changes in voltage, depending on the foods that you eat. These microscopic energy differences can affect the temperature sensations produced by components within certain foods.

When you place a menthol cough drop on your tongue, it produces a cooling sensation. Conversely, a hot chili pepper can give off incredible heat. For this study, lead author Thomas Voets and his colleagues explored how menthol and capsaicin, which is the heat-inducing chemical in chilis, impact cell membranes, or the permeable barriers that surround and protect the contents of cells.

As it turns out, our cell membranes contain cold and heat sensitive chemicals that serve as gates, or entryways, for the voltage shifts

created by ingredients like menthol and cap-
saicin. These two food chemicals modify the
normal state of the cell membrane channels to
either produce the sensation of cold or hot. The
feeling is then carried to our brains through the
central nervous system. It takes a few seconds
for the voltage shifts to occur, which is why you
may not register that you ate a scorching hot
pepper, such as an habanero, until after it has
already filled your mouth with heat. —JV

From "The Principle of Temperature-Dependent Gating in Cold- and Heat-Sensitive TRP Channels"
by Thomas Voets, Guy Droogmans, Ulrich Wissenbach, Annelies Janssens, Veit Flockerzi, and Bernd Nilius
Nature, August 12, 2004

The mammalian sensory system is capable of discriminating thermal stimuli ranging from noxious cold to noxious heat. Principal temperature sensors belong to the TRP cation channel family, but the mechanisms underlying the marked temperature sensitivity of opening and closing ("gating") of these channels are unknown. Here we show that temperature sensing is tightly linked to voltage-dependent gating in the cold-sensitive channel TRPM8 and the heat-sensitive channel TRPV1. Both channels are activated upon depolarization, and changes in temperature result in graded shifts of their voltage-dependent activation curves. The chemical agonists menthol (TRPM8) and capsaicin (TRPV1) function as gating modifiers, shifting activation curves towards physiological membrane potentials. Kinetic analysis of gating at different temperatures indicates that temperature sensitivity in TRPM8 and TRPV1 arises from a tenfold difference in the activation energies associated with voltage-dependent opening and closing. Our results suggest a simple unifying principle that explains both cold and heat sensitivity in TRP channels.

Mammals sense ambient temperature through primary afferent sensory neurons of the dorsal root and trigeminal ganglia.[1, 2] These cells convey thermal information from peripheral tissues to the spinal cord and brain, where the signals are integrated and interpreted, resulting in appropriate reflexive and cognitive responses. The mammalian sensory system is capable of detecting and discriminating thermal stimuli over a broad temperature spectrum, ranging from noxious cold ($< 8°C$) to noxious heat ($> 52°C$), which implies the existence of different types of temperature sensors with distinct thermal sensitivities.[2] Accumulated evidence suggests that the principal temperature sensors in the sensory nerve endings of mammals belong to the transient receptor potential (TRP) superfamily of cation channels.[3, 4] At present, six temperature-sensitive TRP channels (or thermoTRPs)[2] have been described, that together cover almost the entire range of temperatures that mammals are able to sense. Four TRP channels belonging to the TRPV subfamily are activated by heating, with characteristic activation temperatures ranging from warm temperatures (> 25°C for TRPV4; > 31°C for TRPV3)[5-9] to heat (> 43°C for TRPV1)[10] and noxious heat (> 52°C for TRPV2).[11] TRPM8 and TRPA1 (ANKTM1) are activated by cooling, (< 28°C for TRPM8; < 18°C for TRPA1)[12-14]; although the cold-sensitivity of TRPA1 has been disputed.[15]

The origin of the remarkably steep temperature sensitivity of the thermoTRPs is still obscure. Until now, three possible mechanisms for temperature-dependent channel gating have been envisaged.[3] Changes in temperature could lead to the production and binding of channel-activating ligands. Alternatively, the channel protein may undergo temperature-dependent structural rearrangements leading to channel opening. Finally, thermoTRPs may be able to sense changes in membrane tension due to temperature-dependent lipid bilayer rearrangements. However, direct experimental evidence supporting any of these mechanisms is currently lacking.

TRP channels were originally considered as cation channels with little or no voltage sensitivity. This view was in line with the paucity of positively charged residues in the fourth transmembrane domain (S4) (ref. 3), which is known to function as (part of) the voltage sensor in classical voltage-gated K^+, Na^+ and Ca^{2+} channels.[16] Nevertheless, recent studies have demonstrated that TRPM4 and TRPM5, two closely homologous monovalent cation channels, are dually gated by intracellular Ca^{2+} and membrane depolarization.[17-19] Given that the cold- and menthol-sensitive TRPM8 is closely related to TRPM4 and TRPM5, with more

than 40 % similarity at the amino acid level, we investigated whether it displays similar voltage dependence and whether this might be related to its cold sensitivity.

Cold Activation of TRPM8

In whole-cell patch-clamp experiments, cooling to 15°C (Fig. 1a [in the original article]) or application of the cooling agent menthol (Fig. 1b [in the original article]) activated a robust current in human embryonic kidney (HEK) 293 cells transiently transfected with TRPM8, in line with previous reports.[12, 13] Nontransfected or vector-transfected cells were unresponsive to either stimulus. Activation of macroscopic TRPM8 currents by cold and menthol also occurred in cell-free inside-out patches (Fig. 1c, d [in the original article]; data not shown), demonstrating that these stimuli function in a membrane-delimited manner. It should be noted that the temperature-sensitivity of TRPM8 in inside-out patches was shifted towards lower temperatures when compared to whole-cell measurements, which could be due to the loss of a regulatory factor.

A typical feature of TRPM8 currents is the pronounced outward rectification (Fig. 1a–d [in the original article]). Rectification could either be an intrinsic property of the pore or alternatively reflect a voltage-dependent mechanism that closes the channel at negative potentials. Evidence for the latter mechanism was obtained using a classical tail current protocol (Fig. 1e [in the original article]): TRPM8 activates upon depolarization to +120mV and rapidly closes at negative voltages. Notably, the current–voltage relation obtained immediately after the prepulse to +120mV was linear (Fig. 1f [in the original article]), indicating that open TRPM8 channels display an ohmic current–voltage relation. The time-dependent closure of TRPM8 at negative potentials persisted when Ca^{2+} and Mg^{2+} were omitted from the intra- and extracellular solutions, excluding block by divalent cations as a cause of rectification (data not shown). Taken together, our data demonstrate that TRPM8 is a voltage-dependent channel activated by membrane depolarization. Outward rectification arises from the rapid and voltage-dependent closure of the channel at negative voltages.

Next, we asked how the voltage dependence of TRPM8 relates to its function as a cold receptor.[12, 13] To address this, we tested whether articles membrane voltage influences the cold sensitivity of the channel by measuring current activation at different holding potentials during slow cooling of TRPM8-expressing cells. During such cooling protocols we consistently found that current activation at depolarized potentials precedes that at more negative potentials (Fig. 2a, b [in the original article]). At + 100mV, robust outward currents were already activated at 32°C (1,080 ± 230 pA ($n = 12$) versus 69 ± 20 pA ($n = 10$) in non-transfected cells; P < 0.001), whereas inward currents at –80 mV were only discernible upon cooling below ~ 25°C (Fig. 2a, b [in the original article]). Thus, the cold sensitivity of TRPM8 strongly depends on the transmembrane voltage.

Using a voltage step protocol ranging from –120 to +160mV (and in some cases up to +220mV), we

determined how temperature affects the voltage dependence of TRPM8 (Fig. 2c [in the original article]). At 37°C, significant outward currents could only be measured at potentials above +100mV, and the midpoint voltage of activation ($V_{1/2}$) was around +200mV (Fig. 2c–e [in the original article]). Cooling induced a leftward shift of the activation curve resulting in channel activity at more physiological voltages: $V_{1/2}$ decreased by approximately 150mV upon cooling from 37 to 15°C (7.3mV°C^{-1}), and saturated around +25mV between 5 and 10°C (Fig. 2e [in the original article]). From this we conclude that cooling activates TRPM8 by causing a drastic shift of the voltage dependence of activation.

Heat Activation of TRPV1

To test whether a comparable process underlies temperature-dependent gating in a TRP channel with opposite temperature sensitivity, we performed similar experiments in HEK 293 cells expressing TRPV1 (ref. 10). Although TRPV1 was originally described as voltage-independent,[10] some voltage-dependent properties of the channel have been recently described.[20, 21] During slow heating ramps, we observed that activation of TRPV1 at depolarized voltages occurred at significantly lower temperatures than at hyperpolarized voltages (Fig. 3a, b [in the original article]): at –100mV, TRPV1 currents only became prominent at temperatures above 40°C, whereas at +100mV robust outward currents were already present at room temperature (1,742 ± 279 pA (n = 17) versus 59 ± 10 pA (n = 10) in non-transfected cells; $P < 0.001$). Thus, similar to TRPM8, the temperature sensitivity of TRPV1 is strongly dependent on the transmembrane voltage.

We then determined how temperature affects the voltage dependence of TRPV1. At 17°C, significant outward currents could only be measured at potentials above 100mV, and $V_{1/2}$ was around +150mV (Fig. 3c–e [in the original article]). Heating induced a gradual leftward shift of the activation curve, resulting in channel activity at more physiological voltages: $V_{1/2}$ decreased by approximately 200mV upon heating from 17 to 40°C ($9.1mV°C^{-1}$), reaching a value of –50mV between 40 and 45°C (Fig. 3e [in the original article]). Thus, heat-induced activation of TRPV1 is the result of a drastic leftward shift of the voltage dependence of activation.

The Principle of Temperature Sensing

Our present results have important implications when considering possible mechanisms for temperature sensing in TRP channels.[3] First, we found that TRPM8 is activated by cooling in cell-free patches. Similarly, previous work has demonstrated heat-activation of TRPV1 in cell-free patches.[22] These results imply that temperature sensing in both channels is a membrane-delimited process, and argue against temperature-dependent binding of second messengers as a mechanism for channel activation. Second, our results demonstrate that temperature-dependent activation of TRPM8 and TRPV1 is not governed by a single characteristic thermal threshold. Temperature sensitivity is modulated by the transmembrane voltage, and changes in ambient temperature result in graded shifts of the voltage dependence of

channel activation. These results are not in line with the suggestion that channel activation results from a temperature-dependent phase transition of the lipid membrane or a conformational transition (or denaturation) of the channel protein structure,[3] as such processes would predict a single sharp thermal threshold.[23]

As an alternative mechanism, we explored whether temperature sensitivity could be the thermodynamic consequence of differences in the activation energies associated with voltage-dependent channel opening and closing. Given that the time course of TRPM8 and TRPV1 currents during voltage steps was mostly well described with a single exponential function, we employed the simplest, two-state model for a voltage-gated channel:

$$\text{Closed} \underset{\beta(V,T)}{\overset{\alpha(V,T)}{\rightleftharpoons}} \text{Open}$$

The opening and closing rates α and β are related to membrane voltage and temperature according to[16, 24]

$$\alpha = Ae - \frac{E_{a,\,open}}{RT}\, e\, \frac{\delta zFV}{RT} \quad \text{and} \quad \beta = Be - \frac{E_{a,\,close}}{RT}\, e\, \frac{-(1-\delta)zFV}{RT}$$

where $E_{a,open}$ and $E_{a,close}$ represent the activation energies associated with channel opening and closing, R the gas constant (8.31 J mol⁻¹ K⁻¹), T the absolute temperature, z the effective charge associated with voltage-dependent gating, δ is the fraction of z moved in the outward direction, F the Faraday constant (9.65 C 10^{40}Cmol⁻¹),

V the transmembrane voltage and A and B are preexponential factors. According to Eyring rate theory, activation energy and preexponential factor are related to the enthalpic (ΔH) and entropic (ΔS) component of the activation barrier, according to $E_a = \Delta H + RT$ and $A = k_0 e^{\Delta S/R}$ (where k_0 is the frequency factor).[16, 24] Experimental values for z were obtained by fitting the Boltzmann function to the activation curves. Opening and closing rates were obtained from the monoexponential time constant τ of current activation/deactivation and the steady-state P_{open} using the expressions $\alpha = P_{open}/\tau$ and $\beta = (1 - P_{open})/\tau$ (see Supplementary Fig. S1 [in the original article]). Values for α and β as a function of temperature were then displayed in Arrhenius plots (that is, log(rate) versus $1/T$), which allows determination of the activation energy from the slope of the curves.

For TRPM8, the opening rate α was characterized by an $E_{a,open}$ value of 15.7 kJ mol^{-1} corresponding to a 10 °C temperature coefficient (Q_{10}) of 1.2, indicative of a shallow temperature dependence (Fig. 4a [in the original article]). In contrast, the closing rate β was steeply temperature-dependent, reflected in a ~10 times higher value for $E_{a,close}$ of 173 kJ mol^{-1}, which corresponds to a Q_{10} of 9.4 (Fig. 4b [in the original article]). Estimated activation energies were not significantly altered by membrane voltage, which can be appreciated from the parallel Arrhenius plots at different potentials (Fig. 4a, b [in the original article]). Subsequently, we simulated TRPM8 currents using the two-state gating model with the experimentally deduced parameters. Figure 4c [in the original article] shows the simulated temperature dependence of TRPM8 currents at two potentials in response to the cooling ramp used in the experiment of Fig. 2a [in the original article]. The model adequately predicts the cold-induced current activation and the difference in temperature sensitivity at –80 and +100mV (compare Figs. 2b and 4c [in the original article]). Likewise, simulated TRPM8 currents in response to voltage steps at different temperatures (Fig. 4d [in the original article]) were strikingly similar to the experimental data (Fig. 2c [in the original article]). Finally, the model predicted the drastic leftward shift of $V_{1/2}$ upon cooling (dashed line in Fig. 2e [in the original article]), except for a small deviation at temperatures below 10°C, which might reflect channel desensitisation.

In the case of TRPV1, the temperature dependencies of α and β were opposite to those of TRPM8 (Fig. 4e, f [in the original article]): the opening rate α was steeply temperature-dependent ($E_{a,open}$ = 208 kJ mol^{-1}; Q_{10} = 14.8), whereas the closing rate β showed a shallow temperature dependence ($E_{a,close}$ = 23.2 kJ mol^{-1}; Q_{10} = 1.35). Using the two-state model with the experimentally deduced parameters, we could faithfully reproduce the temperature dependence of TRPV1 current at different potentials (Fig. 4g [in the original article]), TRPV1 currents in response to voltage steps at different temperatures (Fig. 4h [in the original article]) and the shift of $V_{1/2}$ as a function of temperature (dashed line in Fig. 3e [in the original article]).

The excellent match between model simulations and experimental results for both TRPM8 and TRPV1 led us to formulate a general principle for temperature sensitivity. Temperature sensitivity occurs whenever the activation energies associated with the opening and closing transitions are sufficiently different. When $E_{a,open}$ $\ll E_{a,close,}$ the open probability of the channel will increase upon cooling, as illustrated by the behaviour of TRPM8 (Fig. 4a–d [in the original article]). On the contrary, the open probability of the channel will increase upon heating when $E_{a,open} \gg E_{a,close,}$ as is the case for TRPV1 (Fig. 4e–h [in the original article]). In most voltage-gated K^+, Ca^{2+} and Na^+ channels the temperature dependence of channel activation and deactivation are similar ($E_{a,open}$ $\approx E_{a,close}$).[16, 25, 26] In these channels, increasing temperature leads to an acceleration of channel gating, without major changes in the steady-state open probability.

Although this principle is rather fundamental, we do not exclude that other thermoTRPs exploit different mechanisms. For example, heat activation of TRPV4 does not occur in cell-free patches,[5, 27] possibly reflecting the necessity of a diffusible messenger. We would also like to point out that a simple two-state model is probably an oversimplification of the full gating intricacies of TRPV1 and TRPM8. Indeed, single-channel measurements of TRPV1 provided evidence for multiple open and closed states.[28] Likewise, we observed that a single exponential function was not always optimal for description of the time dependence of TRPM8, suggesting the presence of more than one open and/or closed state. Nevertheless, the two-state model represents a good approximation of multi-state models as long as the transition with the steepest temperature dependence is rate limiting.

Effect of Ligand Activators

TRPM8 and TRPV1 not only function as temperature sensors, but also as ionotropic receptors for a variety of chemical substances. TRPV1 is directly gated by several chemicals that cause a burning sensation such as vanilloid compounds and protons[10, 22, 29,] as well as by the endocannabinoid anandamide.[30] In contrast, TRPM8 is activated by several plant-derived and synthetic cooling compounds.[12, 13, 31] Our present results raised the question whether these agonists function by modifying the voltage-dependent properties of these channels. To investigate this, we focused on the two best-studied agonists, namely menthol (TRPM8) and capsaicin (TRPV1).

Analogous to previous work,[12, 13] we found that a low dose of menthol (30µM) has little effect on inward TRPM8 current at 34°C, but significantly shifts the cold sensitivity of the channel to higher temperatures (Fig. 5a [in the original article]). The voltage step protocol showed that 30µM menthol caused a strong potentiation of outward currents, a prominent slowing of tail current deactivation and a significant leftward shift of the activation curve (Fig. 5b, c [in the original article]). The menthol-induced leftward shift of the activation curve was independent of temperature (Fig. 5c, d [in the original article]), which explains the enhanced cold sensitivity of TRPM8 in the presence of low doses of the cooling agent. The effect of menthol on the activation curve was dose-dependent, with a half-maximal change in $V_{1/2}$ at 27.4µM (Fig. 5d [in the original article]). Maximal shifts induced by menthol (218mV at 1 µM;

Fig. 5d [in the original article]) were larger than those induced by cooling to 5°C (Fig. 2e [in the original article]), in line with previous findings showing that menthol is a more efficacious TRPM8 agonist than cold.[12]

Capsaicin, the main pungent ingredient of "hot" chili peppers, is one of the most potent chemical activators of TRPV.[10, 22] We found that submicromolar concentrations of capsaicin had a robust effect on outward TRPV1 currents at 24°C, and induced a clear leftward shift of the activation curve (Fig. 6a, b [in the original article]). The effect of capsaicin on the TRPV1 activation curve was dose-dependent, with a halfmaximal shift at 28.5 nM and a maximal change in $V_{1/2}$ of ~200mV (Fig. 6b, c [in the original article]). Note that significant channel desensitization occurs at capsaicin concentrations > 100 nM, which may lead to an underestimation of the shift in $V_{1/2}$ at the highest concentrations tested.

Conclusions

Our results show an unexpected tight link between temperature sensing and voltage-dependent gating in two thermoTRPs with opposite temperature sensitivity. Cold activation of TRPM8 and heat activation of TRPV1 are well described by a single thermodynamic principle, whereby thermosensitivity arises from the difference in activation energies associated with voltage-dependent opening and closing. Chemical agonists of these thermoTRPs function as gating modifiers to mimic and potentiate the thermal responses. At present, the structural determinants of voltage sensing in TRP channels are not known, but the interplay between voltage and temperature sensing implies that any mutational manipulation to the voltage sensor will lead to altered temperature sensitivity. Finally, in a physiological context, our results suggest that the membrane voltage contributes to the fine-tuning of cold- and heat-sensitivity in sensory cells.

1. Julius, D. & Basbaum, A. I. Molecular mechanisms of nociception. *Nature* 413, 203–210 (2001).
2. Patapoutian, A., Peier, A. M., Story, G. M. & Viswanath, V. ThermoTRP channels and beyond: mechanisms of temperature sensation. *Nature Rev. Neurosci.* 4, 529–539 (2003).
3. Clapham, D. E. TRP channels as cellular sensors. *Nature* 426, 517–524 (2003).
4. Voets, T. & Nilius, B. TRPs make sense. *J. Membr. Biol.* 192, 1–8 (2003).
5. Watanabe, H. *et al.* Heat-evoked activation of TRPV4 channels in a HEK293 cell expression system and in native mouse aorta endothelial cells. *J. Biol. Chem.* 277, 47044–47051 (2002).
6. Güler, A. D. *et al.* Heat-evoked activation of the ion channel, TRPV4. *J. Neurosci.* 22, 6408–6414 (2002).
7. Xu, H. *et al.* TRPV3 is a calcium-permeable temperature-sensitive cation channel. *Nature* 418, 181–186 (2002).
8. Smith, G. D. *et al.* TRPV3 is a temperature-sensitive vanilloid receptor-like protein. *Nature* 418, 186–190 (2002).
9. Peier, A. M. *et al.* A heat-sensitive TRP channel expressed in keratinocytes. *Science* 296, 2046–2049 (2002).
10. Caterina, M. J. *et al.* The capsaicin receptor: a heat-activated ion channel in the pain pathway. *Nature* 389, 816–824 (1997).
11. Caterina, M. J., Rosen, T. A., Tominaga, M., Brake, A. J. & Julius, D. A capsaicin-receptor homologue with a high threshold for noxious heat. *Nature* 398, 436–441 (1999).
12. McKemy, D. D., Neuhäusser, W. M. & Julius, D. Identification of a cold receptor reveals a general role for TRP channels in thermosensation. *Nature* 416, 52–58 (2002).
13. Peier, A. M. *et al.* A TRP channel that senses cold stimuli and menthol. *Cell* 108, 705–715 (2002).
14. Story, G. M. *et al.* ANKTM1, a TRP-like channel expressed in nociceptive neurons, is activated by cold temperatures. *Cell* 112, 819–829 (2003).
15. Jordt, S. E. *et al.* Mustard oils and cannabinoids excite sensory nerve fibres through the TRP channel ANKTM1. *Nature* 427, 260–265 (2004).

16. Hille, B. *Ion channels of Excitable Membranes* (Sinauer Associates, Sunderland, Massachusetts, 2001).

17. Launay, P. *et al.* TRPM4 is a Ca^{2+}-activated nonselective cation channel mediating cell membrane depolarization. *Cell* 109, 397–407 (2002).

18. Nilius, B. *et al.* Voltage dependence of the Ca^{2+}-activated cation channel TRPM4. *J. Biol. Chem.* 278, 30813–30820 (2003).

19. Hofmann, T., Chubanov, V., Gudermann, T. &Montell, C. TRPM5 is a voltage-modulated and Ca^{2+}-activated monovalent selective cation channel. *Curr. Biol.* 13, 1153–1158 (2003).

20. Gunthorpe, M. J., Harries, M. H., Prinjha, R. K., Davis, J. B. & Randall, A. Voltage- and time-dependent properties of the recombinant rat vanilloid receptor (rVR1). *J. Physiol. (Lond.)* 525, 747–759 (2000).

21. Vlachova, V. *et al.* Functional role of C-terminal cytoplasmic tail of rat vanilloid receptor 1. *J. Neurosci.* 23, 1340–1350 (2003).

22. Tominaga, M. *et al.* The cloned capsaicin receptor integrates multiple pain-producing stimuli. *Neuron* 21, 531–543 (1998).

23. Marsh, D. General features of phospholipid phase transitions. *Chem. Phys. Lipids* 57, 109–120 (1991).

24. Sigworth, F. J. Voltage gating of ion channels. *Q. Rev. Biophys.* 27, 1–40 (1994).

25. Tiwari, J. K. & Sikdar, S. K. Temperature-dependent conformational changes in a voltage-gated potassium channel. *Eur. Biophys. J.* 28, 338–345 (1999).

26. van Lunteren, E., Elmslie, K. S. & Jones, S. W. Effects of temperature on calcium current of bullfrog sympathetic neurons. *J. Physiol. (Lond.)* 466, 81–93 (1993).

27. Chung, M. K., Lee, H. & Caterina, M. J. Warm temperatures activate TRPV4 in mouse 308 keratinocytes. *J. Biol. Chem.* 278, 32037–32046 (2003).

28. Liu, B., Hui, K. & Qin, F. Thermodynamics of heat activation of single capsaicin ion channels VR1. *Biophys. J.* 85, 2988–3006 (2003).

29. Jordt, S. E., Tominaga, M. & Julius, D. Acid potentiation of the capsaicin receptor determined by a key extracellular site. *Proc. Natl Acad. Sci. USA* 97, 8134–8139 (2000).

30. Zygmunt, P. M. *et al.* Vanilloid receptors on sensory nerves mediate the vasodilator action of anandamide. *Nature* 400, 452–457 (1999).

31. Behrendt, H. J., Germann, T., Gillen, C., Hatt, H. & Jostock, R. Characterization of the mouse coldmenthol receptor TRPM8 and vanilloid receptor type-1 VR1 using a fluorometric imaging plate reader (FLIPR) assay. *Br. J. Pharmacol.* 141, 737–745 (2004).

Every cell in your body contains miniscule power source generators, the mitochondria, which produce chemicals to drive cellular functions. Energy and heat exchanges, therefore, occur all of the time among the cells within our bodies. The cell membrane attempts to regulate this energy and heat to ensure homeostasis, or balance, within the cell.

An antigen is something that produces an immune response. An antigen could be a toxin, such as excess alcohol, a mold spore, or even something as tiny and seemingly innocuous as a single grain of pollen, for those who suffer from hay fever. That is why such a person experiences symptoms like a runny nose and teary eyes, because the body views the antigen as an intruder and attempts to release it through the lymphatic system.

What goes on at the microscopic level, however, has been a mystery. As we all know, no one yet has cured the common cold and flu, much less other viral diseases. The following paper sheds some light on how antigens can invade cells. Thermodynamics appears to be a significant factor. Antigens can take on an "induced fit" that, in essence, allows them to turn into keys to unlock the guarded gates of protein within the cell membrane. The finding could one day lead to better treatments for allergies and disease. These treatments might suppress the antigen's ability to manipulate a healthy cell, or they could strengthen the immune system's intruder response. —JV

"Thermodynamics of T Cell Receptor Binding to Peptide–MHC: Evidence for a General Mechanism of Molecular Scanning"
by J. Jay Boniface, Ziv Reich, Daniel S. Lyons, and Mark M. Davis
***Proceedings of the National Academy of Sciences*, September 1999**

Antigen-dependent activation of T lymphocytes requires T cell receptor (TCR)-mediated recognition of specific peptides, together with the MHC molecules to which they are bound. To achieve this recognition in a reasonable time frame, the TCR must scan and discriminate rapidly between thousands of MHC molecules differing from each other only in their bound peptides. Kinetic analysis of the interaction between a TCR and its cognate peptide–MHC complex indicates that both association and dissociation depend heavily on the temperature, indicating the presence of large energy barriers in both phases. Thermodynamic analysis reveals changes in heat capacity and entropy that are characteristic of protein–ligand associations in which local folding is coupled to binding. Such an "induced-fit" mechanism is characteristic of sequence-specific DNA-binding proteins that must also recognize specific ligands in the presence of a high background of competing elements. Here, we propose that induced fit may endow the TCR with its requisite discriminatory capacity and suggest a model whereby the loosely structured antigen-binding loops of the TCR rapidly explore peptide–MHC complexes on the cell surface until some critical structural complementarity is achieved through localized folding transitions. We further suggest that conformational changes, implicit in this model, may also propagate beyond the TCR antigen-binding site and directly affect self-association of ligated TCRs or TCR–CD3 interactions required for signaling.

The immune system contains two distinct but structurally related antigen receptors, Igs and T cell receptors (TCRs). Unlike Igs, TCRs must recognize their antigens as peptide fragments that are complexed with cell-surface MHC molecules. Developing T cells are selected in the thymus for a minimal ability to recognize self-MHC molecules containing a collection of endogenous peptides (1). After thymic development, peripheral T cells must then distinguish self-MHC molecules containing peptide fragments of antigen from endogenous peptide complexes. Perhaps as a result of this necessity for dual recognition, T cells often have degenerate specificities (2–4), which are rarely seen in mature Ig. Another feature of TCR recognition that distinguishes it from antibodies is that interactions between TCRs and peptide–MHC (pMHC) are often of relatively low affinities and are characterized by unusually slow association and rapid dissociation rates (5).

The molecular basis for these interesting features of TCRs is now emerging. An explanation for crossreactivity was provided recently by Garcia *et al.* (6, 7), who showed poor surface complementarity in a crystal structure of a 2C TCR–pMHC complex. Poor surface complementarity may also explain the relatively low affinities of some TCR–pMHC interactions (7). By comparison to the unligated 2C TCR structure, it was evident that, on binding, large conformational changes occurred in some of the antigen-binding hypervariable (complementarity-determining region; CDR) loops (6, 7). Such "structural plasticity," in turn, suggests that a single TCR may accommodate different pMHC. The conformational change occurring during binding would also seem to explain the unusually slow association rates, as was originally suggested as a possible explanation (8). Further support for this explanation comes from a thermodynamic study by Anton van der Merwe and colleagues (9), who described large energy barriers to association for two class I restricted TCRs. The rapid dissociation rate for TCR–pMHC complexes seems necessary for the coupling of kinetic discrimination and signal transduction (5, 10). For example, in the 2B4 TCR system at 25°C, TCR–pMHC complexes have half-lives of approximately 12, 2, and 0.2 seconds when the peptide was a strong agonist, a weak agonist, or an antagonist, respectively (5). The steep correspondence between complex stability and biological response suggests that an important event in signal transduction occurs on a time scale of seconds, with the caveat that half-lives were measured at 25°C. These facts, together with the observed crossreactivities, indicate that T cells are selected during thymic development to react with endogenous pMHC complexes at

a threshold just below the requirements for peripheral biological response.

The requirement for dual recognition and the presence of structural plasticity in TCRs, however, present another paradox. If a given TCR possesses a minimal but significant affinity for endogenous pMHC complexes and can recognize more than one antigenic peptide, how does a T cell rapidly sort through the irrelevant pMHC complexes, which are present in vast excess, to find and react specifically to antigen? Here, we show that the binding of a particular TCR to its cognate pMHC complex becomes far more rapid as the temperature is increased to 37°C, thereby facilitating the ability of the TCR to sample pMHC complexes over a cell surface. Thermodynamic analysis indicates that binding is coupled to folding transitions, which are probably concentrated but not necessarily confined to the antigen-binding site of the TCR. Propagation of the structural rearrangements induced by binding to regions outside this site might be important for TCR–TCR or TCR–CD3 interactions implicated in signaling.

Materials and Methods

Proteins. The recombinant class II MHC molecule E^k containing a single C-terminal 13-aa biotinylation site was produced as described (11, 12). Briefly, inclusion bodies containing E^k chains were prepared from the BL21(DE3)pLysS strain of *Escherichia coli* by repeated freeze/thaw cycles in 50 mM Tris, pH 8.0/1 mM EDTA/25% (vol/vol) sucrose/1% Triton X-100/1 mg/ml lysozyme. Chains were dissolved individually in

5.8 M guanidine-HCl/50 mM Tris, pH 8.8/2 mM EDTA at less than 1 mg/ml and allowed to oxidize to form disulfide bonds for 5–7 days. After concentration, folding was initiated by combining and diluting subunits to 2 μM in 50 mM sodium phosphate, pH 7.5/25% (vol/vol) glycerol/5 μM reduced glutathione/0.5 mM oxidized glutathione/0.5 mM EDTA/0.1 mM PMSF/1 μg/ml pepstatin/1 μg/ml leupeptin/10 μM moth cytochrome c (MCC) peptide. After 4–5 days of incubation at 4°C, correctly folded MCC–E^k complexes were isolated by immunoaffinity chromatography on a 14.4.4 mAb column. Complexes then were biotinylated enzymatically with the birA enzyme in the presence of protease inhibitors and were size purified to remove aggregates and free biotin. Biotinylation was confirmed by gel-shift assays by using excess streptavidin and was typically greater than 75%. 2B4 TCR was prepared as described (13) as a glycosylphosphatidylinositol-anchored chimera in Chinese hamster ovary cells. Molecules were recovered from cells grown to high density on hollow-fiber bioreactors by phosphatidyl inositol-specific phospholipase C digestion. Heterodimers were purified by tandem immunoaffinity chromatography on an anti-α-chain column (A2B4) followed by an anti-β-chain column (H57). Protein was then size purified on a Superdex-200 FPLC column immediately before BIAcore analyses. Quantification was made by using an extinction coefficient (280 nm) of 1.3 ml·mg^{-1}·cm^{-1}.

BIAcore Analysis. The BIAcore streptavidin chip was prewashed with two short pulses of 0.05% SDS, and biotinylated MCC–E^k was immobilized to an

approximate level of 3,500 resonance units. Soluble 2B4 TCR binding was monitored at a flow rate of 15 μl/min in PBS containing 0.005 % P-20 detergent (BIAcore, Uppsala). PBS was filtered and degassed before use. Binding curves were fit by using the Marquardt–Levenberg nonlinear least squares algorithm provided in the BIAEVALUATION 2.1 package. A BIAcore1000 was used to collect data from 20°C to 37°C. Because of its stability at lower temperatures, a BIAcore2000 was used to collect data from 10°C to 20°C. At 20°C, kinetic parameters on the two devices were identical. BIAcore-binding data generally do not seem to be limited by mass transport in this system (8). Potential mass-transport regions of BIAcore curves, when present, were not included in the analysis. Great care was taken to remove existing aggregates (above) before analysis, and the purified individual molecules (2B4 TCR and MCC–E^k) do not self-associate at the concentrations tested (14). Calculated dissociation-rate constants showed little or no dependence on analyte concentration. Calculated association-rate constants showed some analyte concentration dependence (as much as 2- to 3-fold across a 10-fold range in analyte concentration). Calculated rate constants at each analyte concentration and for each experiment were averaged to give the combined data set (see Fig. 2 [in the original article]). χ^2 values for individual fits were typically less than 1.0.

Thermodynamic Analysis. The equilibrium-association constants (K) were calculated from the ratio of the rate constants (k_a/k_d). Thermodynamic parameters were determined by calculating $\Delta G°$ values (free energy change) by using $\Delta G° = -RT\ln K_T$ and fitting them as a function of temperature (T) according to

$$\Delta G°_T = \Delta H°_{T_0} + \Delta C°_p(T - T_0) - T\Delta S°_{T_0} - T\Delta C°_p \ln(T/T_0), \tag{1}$$

where $\Delta H°_{T_0}$ (enthalpy change), $\Delta S°_{T_0}$ (entropy change), and $\Delta C°_p$ (heat-capacity change) are used as fitting parameters (15). $\Delta C°_p$ was assumed to be independent of temperature; inclusion of a $\Delta C°_p/dT$ term in the analysis did not improve the quality of the fits and gave larger standard errors for the returned parameters. Such insensitivity of $\Delta C°_p$ to the temperature in the physiological range is consistent with processes dominated by the hydrophobic effect, such as an induced fit (16). Eq. 1, rearranged to include kinetic terms, was used to fit some of the data (see Fig. 2 [in the original article]). $\Delta H°$ and $T\Delta S°$ plots (see Fig. 3B [in the original article]) were made by using

$$\Delta H°_T = \Delta H°_{T_0} + \Delta C°_P (T - T0) \tag{2}$$

and

$$\Delta S°_T = \Delta S°_{T0} + \Delta C°p \ln(T/T_0). \tag{3}$$

Model Building of the 2B4–MCC–E^k Complex. The 2B4 TCR α- and β-chains were modeled separately by using 2C TCR as a template (coordinates kindly provided by K. C. Garcia, Stanford Univ., Stanford, CA, and I. A. Wilson, The Scripps Research Institute, La Jolla, CA). Sequence identity between target and

template was 60.6% (α) and 65.6% (β). Sequence alignment, model building, energy minimization, and three-dimensional profile analysis were all made by using the SWISS-MODEL automated comparative protein modeling server (refs. 17–19; www.expasy.ch/swissmod/SWISS-MODEL.html). After this step, the two chains were combined, and the structure was energy minimized further by using GROMOS96 (W. F. van Gunsteren; BIOMOS b.v, Laboratory of Physical Chemistry, Eidgenössische Technische Hochschule Zentrum, Zurich). Computations were made *in vacuo* by using the 43B1 parameters set. The energy minimized 2B4 heterodimer, along with its ligand, MCC–E^k (Protein Data Bank ID code 1IEA; with MCC residues 88–103 substituted for the original peptide), was then superimposed on 2C–K^b template, and the complex was energy minimized by GROMOS96.

Accessible Surface Areas. Accessible surface areas were calculated with the program NACCESS (20) by using a 1.4-Å probe sphere.

Results and Discussion

The class II MHC molecule E^k complexed to an antigenic peptide fragment of MCC (residues 88–103) was attached to a streptavidin sensor chip (BIACore) via a single biotin positioned at the C terminus of the MHC α-chain. Binding of the $\alpha\beta$ TCR, 2B4, which recognizes and specifically interacts with this complex (5), was then measured at various temperatures by surface plasmon resonance. Fig. 1 [in the original article] illustrates the large temperature dependence of the overall reaction.

The kinetics in both directions becomes more rapid as the temperature is increased, leading to a faster approach to equilibrium.

Fig. 2 [in the original article] summarizes the temperature dependence of the association-rate (Fig. 2A [in the original article]) and dissociation-rate (Fig. 2B [in the original article]) constants. Slow association kinetics (owing to a large association activation energy) and steep temperature dependence, for both phases, are evident. As also shown, the plots are not linear but have a gentle, but clear, concave up (k_d) and down (k_a) curvature, indicating, in addition to a deviation from a simple reaction mechanism, a significant heat-capacity change (ΔC_p°) in both phases (463 ± 53 and −200 ± 48 cal·mol^{-1}·K^{-1}, respectively; 1 cal = 4.18 J). These data cannot be explained by aggregation, because great care was taken to eliminate aggregates before analysis (see *Materials and Methods*) and because neither molecule alone aggregates at these concentrations (14). Owing to the marked variation of k_d with temperature, the reaction half-life ($t_{1/2}$) also has a steep temperature dependence, decreasing from 240 sec at 10°C to almost 3 sec at 37°C (Fig. 2B *Inset* [in the original article]). This last value (3 sec) is much smaller than those reported for TCR–pMHC interactions (reviewed in ref. 5), most of which have been measured at 25°C. It is also much faster than the $t_{1/2}$ determined by Sykulev *et al.* (21) for the 2C TCR and one of its ligands at 37°C (46 sec). However, the 2C TCR–pMHC interaction is of unusually high affinity, and the same interaction measured at 25°C is five times slower (21), consistent with the ratio observed here. As it is more typical of TCRs, the $t_{1/2}$ value for the 2B4 TCR may be useful in models concerning ligand discrimination (10, 22) and self-association (14). We note, however, that the $t_{1/2}$ values reported here are likely to be shorter than those prevailing *in vivo* because of a reduction in the TCR's translational and rotational freedom on the cell surface and the presence of coreceptors that interact and stabilize the ternary complex. The increase in the reaction on-and-off rates with temperature is also compatible with the proposed model of serial engagement, whereby a single pMHC complex could interact transiently with and trigger a large number of TCRs (23).

The thermodynamics of the 2B4–MCC–E^k association is summarized in Fig. 3 [in the original article]. Of the parameters shown (Fig. 3A [in the original article]), of particular interest is a large negative $\Delta C°_{p\,assoc}$, which is indicative of the removal of substantial amounts of nonpolar surface area from solvent on binding. It also gives rise to thermodynamics that typify an entropy–enthalpy compensation process (i.e., with $|\Delta C°_{p\,assoc}| \gg |\Delta S°_{assoc}|$) in which enthalpy contributes favorably to the interaction throughout the entire temperature range studied (Fig. 3B [in the original article]). Entropy, on the other hand, mostly opposes association and makes a favorable contribution only at low temperatures (below 290 K).

For rigid-body associations, observed changes in heat capacity often can be predicted very accurately based solely on the amount of surface area buried on complex formation (see ref. 24 and references therein).

We have calculated $\Delta C^\circ_{p\,assoc}$ for two known TCR–pMHC complex structures and for a model of 2B4–MCC–E^k. As indicated (Table 1 [in the original article]), all three complexes bury roughly the same amount of nonpolar and polar surfaces, yielding similar $DC^\circ_{p\,assoc}$ of approximately -250 cal·mol^{-1}·K^{-1}. Predicted values are thus only one-half to one-third as large as the experimentally determined value of -663 cal·mol^{-1}·K^{-1} for the 2B4 TCR and its ligand. The large discrepancy between calculated and observed $|\Delta C^\circ_p|$ argues against a rigid-body association and indicates that binding involves an induced fit. In this case, the excess $|\Delta C^\circ_p|$ results from the burial of additional nonpolar surfaces through the folding transitions concomitant to binding.

An induced-fit mechanism is supported further and more definitively by a dissection of the total entropy change ΔS°_{assoc} of the 2B4–MCC–E^k association. ΔS°_{assoc} includes several contributions and, for protein–ligand interactions, may be expressed as

$$\Delta S^\circ_{assoc} = \Delta S^\circ_{HE} + \Delta S^\circ_{tr} + \Delta S^\circ_{other}, \qquad [4]$$

where ΔS°_{HE} and ΔS°_{tr} correspond to entropy changes arising from the hydrophobic effect and changes in the molecules' rotational and translational entropy, respectively, and ΔS°_{other} includes any other entropic effects (e.g., changes in vibrational or conformational entropy) and is assumed to be temperature independent (24). For rigid-body associations, contributions arising from ΔS°_{other} are usually very small, and ΔS°_{assoc} is determined by only ΔS°_{HE} and ΔS°_{tr} (24). For an induced fit, however, a significant negative ΔS°_{other} term, amounting to

the loss in conformational entropy on structure formation, should be present. For the 2B4–MCC–E^k
association at T_s (290 K; where $\Delta S°_{assoc} = 0$; Fig. 3 [in
the original article]), we calculate (by using equation 3
in ref. 24) $\Delta S°_{HE}$ to be 256 entropy units. Because $\Delta S°_{tr}$
is relatively constant and, for bimolecular protein–protein
associations, averages to –50 ± 10 entropy units
(24–26), summation of these two contributions leaves a
substantial unfavorable $\Delta S°_{other}$ term of –206 entropy
units. This value of $\Delta S°_{other}$ falls in the midrange of
values reported by Spolar and Record (24) for processes
known to couple local or long-range folding to site-
specific binding. The low T_s (290 K) determined here is
likewise a value typical of such processes (24). Finally,
the number of residues that change their conformation
on binding can be estimated from $\Delta S°_{other}$ (24) and, for
the reaction investigated, is calculated to be 36.

The binding of 2B4 to MCC–E^k therefore fits a
thermodynamic signature characteristic of reactions
involving an induced fit. Although folding transitions,
implicit in this model, may occur anywhere in the MHC
or the TCR, they are most likely to be dominated by the
TCR hypervariable loops (CDRs), which seem likely to
be inherently flexible binding interfaces. Some of these
loops have indeed been shown by crystallographic
studies (6, 7) to undergo substantial rearrangements on
binding. In contrast, the structure of pMHC molecules
changes very little when bound to the TCR (7, 27).
Thus, we propose that the TCR CDR loops are particularly flexible in the free state and become ordered only
on binding as a result of localized folding transitions.

Results consistent with the formation of structure during TCR–pMHC binding also were obtained recently by thermodynamic analyses for two different class I restricted TCRs (9). Folding, as determined here, is substantial and is estimated to involve about 36 residues. This number of residues undergoing conformational changes on binding is significantly larger than indicated by x-ray analyses of the bound and free 2C TCR (7). Thus, in general, the values derived here suggest that TCRs may be significantly less ordered in solution than in the crystalline state. The extensive change in conformational entropy measured here could also arise, in part, from subtle rearrangements that propagate beyond the antigen-binding loops. Of note in this regard is the fact that small shifts in VαVβ pairing were observed in the 2C TCR on binding (6, 7). Such structural shifts or other subtle conformational rearrangements could potentially enhance the interface complementarity required for the self-association of ligated TCRs (14) or TCR–CD3 interactions required for signaling.

In trying to understand TCR-mediated recognition in the context of an induced-fit model, appealing parallels can be drawn to the recognition of DNA by site-specific binding proteins. Like the TCR, DNA-binding proteins must rapidly discriminate between numerous competing and chemically similar elements, and the presence of an induced fit has been shown in several such proteins (24). In these cases, recognition does not follow a rigid alignment of preexisting complementary surfaces. Instead, regions in the protein (and, in some cases, in the DNA), which are unstructured in the free state, fold on binding to create key parts of the contact interface. This "on-site" construction of the protein–DNA interface indicates that the final conformation will depend strongly on the DNA sequence bound, as indeed has been observed (e.g., refs. 28–30). As expected, engagement of the binding protein with the DNA during scanning is mediated by nonspecific electrostatic interactions.

Analogously, the TCR must discriminate amongst thousands of chemically similar pMHCs on the cell surface through transient interactions that are relatively insensitive to the peptide antigen. These interactions are most likely made with epitopes located over the MHC helices. Mutagenesis and structural data indicating a common, peptide-independent orientation of all TCRs over the pMHC ligand (5, 7) are consistent with such a model. Once a cognate complex is found, the free energy of binding could drive local rearrangements in the CDRs, a process by which surface complementarity is maximized and complex stability is enhanced. As noted above, this structural adaptation may, in principle, be ligand dependent; different structures may form on different pMHC ligands. That this model may well be the case was suggested earlier by Ehrich *et al.* (31), who found that the pattern of MHC mutants that disrupted recognition by a particular TCR varied markedly when different peptides were recognized. More recently, Mason (32) has suggested that each TCR must be inherently able to interact with many peptides to account for thymic selection and crossreactivities (e.g., refs. 2–4). Such plasticity, as noted by Garcia *et al.* (6, 7) would give rise to a wide spectrum of complexes of various stabilities and lifetimes and, hence, may lead to markedly different signaling events, as has also been observed in this system (10, 33, 34). We further suggest that the energy necessary to form encounter pairs during the search mode is provided predominantly by the CDR loops directly contacting the MHC moiety. Stable complex formation, on the other hand, most likely involves CDRs engaged in peptide recognition, such as the CDR3 loops and, hence, is ligand dependent.

An interesting feature of αβ TCRs is that their most hypervariable loops (CDR3) are very constrained in size when compared with those of Ig heavy chains. Thus, the CDR3 of human TCR α- or β-chains have a median length of 9 aa and a range of 6–12 aa (35). This median length is compared with a one of 12 aa and a range of 3–25 aa observed for Ig heavy-chain CDR3s (35). This selection for certain CDR3 lengths in αβ TCRs may reflect a compromise. A minimum number of residues are clearly needed to afford specificity and conformational flexibility. On the other hand, the energetic costs associated with structure formation set a limit to this number, above which the expenditure of free energy would become too costly to sustain the low-affinity-based scanning of the MHC surfaces. In contrast, the length diversity seen in Ig heavy-chain CDR3s may be the result of the fact that there is no need for a scanning function, because there is no commonality between most ligands and no preferred binding orientation. It is also interesting to note that Ig CDR loops are optimized in a preferred high-affinity conformation through somatic hypermutation as an immune response matures. Therefore, the necessity for an induced fit in the already selected, *matured* forms becomes significantly reduced. Consequently, in many cases in which mature antibody–antigen interactions have been studied, evidence for an induced fit is lacking (36–41), and, in cases where it has been described (42–44), structural changes are significantly smaller than those seen in the 2C TCR (7) and those predicted here. That an induced-fit mechanism may be more prevalent in nonsomatically mutated antibodies has been elegantly established by Wedemayer *et al.* (45), who have shown that a nonmutated antibody to a hapten binds by an induced-fit mechanism, whereas a mutated form does not.

Recently, Willcox et al. (9) described temperature effects similar to those reported here and, in particular, a striking loss of entropy on binding for two TCRs that recognize class I MHC ligands. These data, together with existing structural data and the similarity in thermodynamics of binding in TCRs and DNA-binding proteins, suggest that an induced-fit mechanism may be general to systems that require the rapid scanning of many similar molecular entities.

ABBREVIATIONS

TCR, T cell receptor; CDR, complementarity-determining region; pMHC, peptide–MHC; MCC, moth cytochrome c.

References

1. Saito, T. & Watanabe, N. (1998). *Crit. Rev. Immunol.* 18, 359–370.
2. Bhardwaj, V., Kumar, V., Geysen, H. M., & Sercarz, E. E. (1993). *J. Immunol.* 151, 5000–5010.
3. Evavold, B. D., Sloan-Lanchaster, J., Wilson, K. J., Rothbard, J. B., & Allen, P. M. (1995). *Immunity* 2, 655–663.

4. Wucherpfennig, K. W. & Strominger, J. L. (1995). *Cell* 80, 695–705.

5. Davis, M. M., Boniface, J. J., Reich, Z., Lyons, D., Hampl, J., Arden, B., & Chien, Y. (1998). *Annu. Rev. Immunol.* 16, 523–544.

6. Garcia, K. C. & Teyton, L. (1998). *Curr. Opin. Biotechnol.* 4, 338–343.

7. Garcia, K. C., Degano, M., Pease, L. R., Huang, M., Peterson, P. A., Teyton, L., & Wilson, I. A. (1998). *Science* 279, 1166–1172.

8. Matsui, K., Boniface, J. J., Steffner, P., Reay, P. A., & Davis, M. M. (1994). *Proc. Natl. Acad. Sci. USA* 91, 2862–2866.

9. Willcox, B. E., Gao, G. F., Wyer, J. R., Ladbury, J. E., Bell, J. I., Jakobsen, B. K., & Anton van der Merwe, P. (1999). *Immunity* 10, 357–365.

10. Rabinowitz, J. D., Beeson, C., Lyons, D. S., Davis, M. M., & McConnell, H. M. (1996). *Proc. Natl. Acad. Sci. USA* 93, 1401–1405.

11. Altman, J. D., Reay, P. A., & Davis, M. M. (1993). *Proc. Natl. Acad. Sci. USA* 90, 10330–10334.

12. Boniface, J. J., Rabinowitz, J. D., Wulfing, C., Hampl, J., Reich, Z., Altman, J. D., Kantor, R. M., Beeson, C., McConnell, H. M., & Davis, M. M. (1998). *Immunity* 9, 459–466.

13. Lin, A. Y., Devaux, B., Green, A., Sagerstrom, C., Elliott, J. F., & Davis, M. M. (1990). *Science* 249, 677–679.

14. Reich, Z., Boniface, J. J., Lyons, D. S., Borochov, N., Wachtel, E. J., & Davis, M. M. (1997). *Nature (London)* 387, 617–620.

15. Yoo, S. H. & Lewis, M. S. (1995). *Biochemistry* 34, 632–638.

16. Ha, J.-H., Spolar, R. S., & Record, M. T., Jr. (1989). *J. Mol. Biol.* 209, 801–816.

17. Peitsch, M. C. (1995). *Bio/Technology* 13, 658–660.

18. Peitsch, M. C. (1996). *Biochem. Soc. Trans.* 24, 274–279.

19. Guex, N. & Peitsch, M. C. (1997). *Electrophoresis* 18, 2714–2723.

20. Hubbard, S. J. & Thornton, J. M. (1993) in *NACCESS* (Univ. Coll., London).

21. Sykulev, Y., Brunmark, A., Tsomides, T. J., Kageyama, S., Jackson, M., Peterson, P. A., & Eisen, H. N. (1994). *Proc. Natl. Acad. Sci. USA* 91, 11487–11491.

22. McKeithan, T. W. (1995). *Proc. Natl. Acad. Sci. USA* 92, 5042–5046.

23. Valitutti, S., Muller, S., Cella, M., Padovan, E., & Lanzavecchia, A. (1995). *Nature* (London) 375, 148–151.

24. Spolar, R. S. & Record, T. R., Jr. (1994). *Science* 263, 777–784.

25. Finkelstein, A. V. & Janin, J. (1989). *Protein Eng.* 3, 13.

26. Janin, J. & Chothia, C. (1978). *Biochemistry* 17, 2943–2948.

27. Ding, Y. H., Smith, K. J., Garboczi, D. N., Utz, U., Biddison, W. E., & Wiley, D. C. (1998). *Immunity* 8, 403–411.

28. Winkler, F. K. (1993). *EMBO J.* 12, 1781–1795.

29. Clarke, N. D., Beamer, L. J., Goldberg, H. R., Berkower, C., & Pabo, C. O. (1991). *Science* 254, 267–270.

30. O'Neil, K. T., Hoess, R. H., & DeGrado, W. F. (1990). *Science* 249, 774–778.

31. Ehrich, E. W., Devaux, B., Rock, E. P., Jorgensen, J. L., Davis, M. M., & Chien, Y. (1993). *J. Exp. Med.* 178, 713–722.

32. Mason, D. (1998). *Immunol. Today* 9, 395–404.

33. Lyons, D. S., Lieberman, S. A., Hampl, J., Boniface, J. J., Chien, Y., Berg, L. J., & Davis, M. M. (1996). *Immunity* 5, 53–61.

34. Kersh, E. N., Shaw, A. S., & Allen, P. M. (1998). *Science* 281, 572–575.

35. Rock, E. P., Sibbald, P. R., Davis, M. M., & Chien, Y.-h. (1994). *J. Exp. Med.* 179, 323–328.

36. Murphy, K. P., Xie, D., Garcia, K. C., Amzel, L. M., & Freire, E. (1993). *Proteins* 15, 113–120.

37. Bhat, T. N., Bentley, G. A., Boulot, G., Greene, M. I., Tello, D., Dall'Acqua, W., Souchon, H., Schwarz, F. P., Mariuzza, R. A., & Poljak, R. J. (1994). *Proc. Natl. Acad. Sci. USA* 91, 1089–1093.

38. Hibbits, K. A., Gill, D. S., & Willson, R. C. (1994). *Biochemistry* 33, 3584–3590.

39. Murphy, K. P., Freire, E., & Patterson, Y. (1995). *Proteins* 21, 8390.

40. Fields, B. A., Goldbaum, F. A., Dall'Acqua, W., Malchiodi, E. L., Cauerhff, A., Schwarz, F. P., Ysern, X., Poljak, R. J., & Mariuzza, R. A. (1996). *Biochemistry* 35, 15494–15503.

41. Tsumoto, K., Ogasahara, K., Ueda, Y., Watanabe, K., Yutani, K., & Kumagai, I. (1996). *J. Biol. Chem.* 271, 32612–32616.

42. Schulze-Gahmen, U., Rini, J. M., & Wilson, I. A. (1993). *J. Mol. Biol.* 234, 1098–1118.

43. Stanfield, R. L., Takimoto-Kamimura, M., Rini, J. M., Profy, A. T., & Wilson, I. A. (1993). *Structure* 1, 8393.

44. Rini, J. M., Schulze-Gahmen, U., & Wilson, I. A. (1992). *Science* 255, 959–965.

45. Wedemayer, G. J., Patten, P. A., Wang, L. H., Schultz, P. G., & Stevens, R. C. (1997). *Science* 276, 1665–1669.

Humans create most machines in their own image. We take in a lot of energy and release a lot of waste matter, be it food or water related,

or the carbon dioxide that we exhale with each breath. While machines do not necessarily breathe, the underlying thermodynamics of their functions is comparable to the thermodynamics found within our own bodies.

Some theorists have suggested that plant processes, such as photosynthesis, would provide a better thermodynamic model in creating machines and in tapping alternate energy sources, such as solar energy. Since plants bind energy from the Sun into the chemical potential energy of components found within the leaves and stems, the energy cycle does not yield a great deal of entropy, especially when compared to the waste matter and heat released when the energy within fossil fuels is released and dispersed.

Most plants hardly seem like great reservoirs of energy, however, beyond the food value of certain fruits and vegetables. In this Science News article, author Susan Milius describes a novel discovery—some plants generate heat, and in quantities greater than any other known plant or animal of comparable size and density. Since heat is energy, and humans are good at duplicating natural processes in the world of mechanics, it will be interesting to see how a heat-producing plant like dead-horse arum might be used in future research projects. —JV

"Warm-Blooded Plants? OK, There's No Blood, But They Do Make Their Own Heat"
by Susan Milius
Science News, December 13, 2003

"The dead-horse arum of Corsica looks and smells like the south end of a horse that died going north," says Roger Seymour. He's actually talking about a plant, and a more prosaic soul might add that it belongs to the same family as calla lilies and jack-in-the-pulpits. Seymour is a zoologist, and the plants he studies show an animalistic feature: They can generate body heat Most plants, including calla lilies and jack-in-the-pulpits, simply assume the ambient temperature because their metabolic reactions hum along so gently that they don't give off bursts of heat. The dead-horse arum, however, belongs to the group of several hundred plant species scattered among some 10 families that can rev up their own furnaces. That heat can launch strong odors, like those of a dumpster in August. In winter, warm flowers can melt snow.

The dead-horse arum outdoes all the others, says Seymour, who's at the University of Adelaide in Australia. The plant's flesh-pink blooms produce more heat than does any other known plant or any animal considered in its entirety. Scientists have measured higher rates of bodily heat production only in the flight muscles of some insects and, possibly, the brown fat of hamsters.

Descriptions of remarkable heat-making plant species date back more than 200 years, but scientists are still discovering new facets of the phenomenon, sometimes hidden in plain sight. Current research about the biochemistry behind plant heat may someday change the way people deal with heat. The pattern of heating power in the botanical family tree intrigues evolutionists searching for traits of ancient flowering plants. And, this winter, two research teams have presented new research on what good this heating does for a plant.

Kidnappers

All the plant tissues so far found to warm themselves have reproductive functions, and Seymour sees common themes among the hot species' sex lives. They tend toward large blooms, which have a low surface-to-volume ratio favoring heat retention. In many of these blooms, the female organs mature before the male parts, requiring the plant to briefly kidnap pollinators to make its pollination system work.

Consider the dead-horse arum, *Helicodiceros muscivorus*. In spring on islands in the Mediterranean, these plants send up blooms with a central, fingerlike projection in front of a rounded dish of tissue, or spathe, several inches wide. When the plant first blooms, the finger radiates heat, which sends out strong aromas. Female blowflies soon swarm over the bloom.

Botanists have speculated that the stench represents step 1 in an entrapment scheme, attracting blowflies under the false pretense that there's nice dead flesh available as a nursery for their eggs. Tests bear that out, reported Marcus C. Stensmyr of the Swedish University of Agricultural Sciences in Alnarp and his colleagues in the Dec. 12, 2002 *Nature*. Several dominant compounds, called oligosulfides, showed up in both the stink of the flower and in that of a dead seagull. A study of nerve responses of blowfly antennae showed that the flies respond similarly to the composites of compounds that make up the scents, so they don't seem to be able to tell a flower from a dead gull on the basis of smell alone.

In nature, once flies buzz in to explore the dead-horse–arum bloom, many crawl down into the pocket where the spathe narrows to surround the base of the finger. That pocket contains a band of male florets above a band of female florets. Spines and filaments at the entrance to the pocket imprison the flies.

During the first day that a dead-horse arum blooms, female florets have matured enough to receive pollen, but male florets aren't releasing it. The flies, however, may carry pollen they picked up from a previous adventure in another, earlier-blooming plant. As the flies scramble around in the pocket, trying to escape, they dust that pollen onto female florets.

By the next day, the female organs have lost their receptivity but the male parts have matured. The trapped insects then pick up pollen. The blockade of spines withers, so the flies can at last squeeze up out of the pocket. They then carry the new pollen to the next arum, should they fall for the same trick again.

Self-Control

Seymour reminisces that he first learned about heat-generating flowers several decades ago, when a friend brought the large fingerlike projection of a self-heating flower, *Philodendron selloum*, as a conversation piece to a California party. The structure was warm to the touch and looked more like a mammal's reproductive organ than a plant's.

Seymour was so taken with the structure that he savaged philodendron blooms in his mother's garden to get specimens for measuring heat generation. Thus began the project that first documented a new twist in a few self-warming plants.

While the dead-horse arum and most other self-heating plants produce heat on a preset schedule, regardless of the air temperature, *P. selloum* manages something more sophisticated: It regulates its heat generation to keep its flower temperature approximately steady, Seymour and his colleagues reported in 1972.

Growing outdoors, *P. selloum* keeps its blooms between about 30°C and 36°C. In lab tests, the flowers manage to stay in this range even when experimenters chill the air to 4°C.

Those experiments also revealed that most of the plant's heat comes from a band of tiny, sterile male flowers located between the fertile male and female flowers on the bloom's fingerlike projection. The sterile blooms shut down heat production when air temperature reaches about 37°C.

Like the dead-horse arum, this philodendron in its native Brazil lures insects inside. The philodendron's spathe closes over scarab beetles for only 12 hours. Yet the beetles remain for some 22 hours. While in the bloom, they mate, feed, and brush pollen onto female flowers. At the end of the beetles' stay, they pick up pollen from just-matured male flowers and fly off to another bloom.

The eastern skunk cabbage (*Symplocarpus foetidus*) in North America and Asia also keeps warm, independent of air temperature, Roger Knutson reported in 1974. The insect-pollinated plant flowers early in the year, sometimes by New Year's Day in mid-Atlantic states. Its bloom, a thick-walled, teardrop-shaped spathe surrounding a fat stub covered with florets, can melt holes in the snow cover.

Skunk cabbages can bloom inside a snowbank and create their own ice caves. "You can break through the snow and look into these fantastic spaces," Seymour says.

In experiments at air temperatures around 15°C, the inner core averaged some 9° higher. When the air temperature dropped to –15°C though, the fingerlike projections reached temperatures 30° higher than the air. "Some mammals can't even do that well," says Seymour.

In 1996, Seymour and his University of Adelaide colleague Paul Schultze-Motel reported that the Asian sacred lotus (*Nelumbo nucifera*) could also regulate its flower temperature. The species is hardly rare or unfamiliar. It grows widely on both sides of the Atlantic Ocean, but no one had previously tested it for temperature regulation. The Adelaide team found that as environmental temperatures dropped as low as 10°C, flower temperatures stayed between 30°C and 36°C.

The researchers decided to see whether day-night cycling influences the lotus' temperature control, as it does in some other plants. The team covered individual lotus blooms with translucent jackets made from inverted wine-bottle coolers and reversed the normal temperature pattern for night and day. The flowers tracked the temperature instead of the light, Seymour and his colleagues reported in 1998.

The dead-horse arum maintains a relatively stable bloom temperature, but the plant isn't a true temperature regulator, says Marc Gibernau of Paul Sabatier University in Toulouse, France. He, Seymour, and Kikukatsu Ito of Iwate University in Morioka, Japan, found that heating related more to time than air temperature, they report in the December 2003 *Functional Ecology*.

There's only one other plant that's been identified as regulating heat production. It's a South American species, *Xanthosoma robustum*, that's related to the dead-horse arum, philodendron, and skunk cabbage. *X. robustum* has received less attention so far.

Furnace Design

The past 5 years have shaken up the study of the chemistry of hot plants by adding a new heat-generating pathway for scientists to probe. Since 1932, physiologists have known about one heat-making pathway, which is a secondary process for respiration. By the 1970s, physiologists had linked the slow-heat burns of arums with a jump in activity in this pathway. An enzyme in the pathway, alternative oxidase or AOX, occurs only in plant cells, where it's located in the cell powerhouses called mitochondria.

Mammal mitochondria can blast out heat, too, but they rely on what's called uncoupling proteins, UCPs.

In 1997, a European research team reported similar chemistry in potatoes. Cold prompted activity of a gene making what looked like aversion of a mammalian UCP rather than an AOX, said Maryse Laloi of the Max Planck Institute for Molecular Plant Physiology in Golm, Germany.

Ito then began searching for UCPs in skunk cabbages. In 1999, he reported finding genes encoding two UCPs. A temperature drop activated these genes only in the floret-holding stub. The UCPs and AOX seem to function for heat generation simultaneously, he and his colleagues reported at the Plant Biology 2003 meeting in Hawaii in June. "Now, we have to reconsider the functions of two different thermogenic reactions," says Ito.

Since 2001, Ito and his Iwate colleagues—with support from the Japanese government—have been searching for the temperature sensor and other compounds that operate in the skunk cabbage's heat production. The researchers have figured out the basic protocol that the plant follows, says Ito. "We call it 'the skunk cabbage algorithm.'"

Ito has applied for a patent on this protocol and isn't releasing the details. "This sort of biological algorithm could be used as a new brain to control nonbiological devices, such as air conditioners," he says. The standard program controlling an air conditioner was invented more than 60 years ago. The system used by a skunk cabbage, "which is a typical chaotic system, is totally different," he says. Ito's team has recently succeeded in operating an artificial heater with this algorithm. "I really think we can learn a lot from skunk cabbages," he says.

What's Hot

The majority of the hundreds of plants known to generate heat sprout from ancient lineages at the base of the botanical family tree, observes Leonard Thien of Tulane University in New Orleans. Self heating may have been an early innovation that arose soon after the invention of flowering.

Evolutionists are looking at thermogenesis as they reevaluate traits in these old lines. "At the moment, a great deal of discussion is under way to decide upon the state of various characters," says Thien.

For example, heat generation has turned up in certain plants of these ancient lineages of flowering plants: the magnolias, Dutchman's pipes, star anises, custard apples, and water lilies. Heat-generating flowers include the darling of 19th-century aquatic gardens, the Amazon water lily (*Victoria amazonica*).

Thien says that preliminary results suggest that at least one other ancient family includes a self heater, but he won't say which one until he double-checks his results next spring.

The most ancient family that Thien has tested is *Amborellaceae*. Only one member remains, a scrub in New Caledonia, and it shows no sign of heat generation, he and his team report.

Moreover, there's no sharp boundary for the evolutionary disappearance of thermogenesis. The trait does show up in a few lineages of moderately recent origin, such as the arums, the palms, and a related family sometimes called the Panama-hat palms. The Asian sacred lotus represents the highest branch on the botanical family tree that shows heat generation.

The Bottom Line

Study of the evolution of heat generation raises questions about what benefits it might bring, or once brought, to a plant. The trait's absence among the newest plant families suggests that its value has declined as modem plants developed.

Biologists first proposed that heat helps spread the plants' insect-attracting odors. In contrast, one recent finding suggests that heat might make a plant more closely resemble a dead animal because microbial processes in a carcass raise its temperature.

Heating an artificially scented plant restored a fading bloom's capacity to lure insects into its pocket. "This is the first time it has been proved that this heating function of the plant is important, with scent, for guiding the pollinators," says Anna Maria Angioy of the University of Cagliari in Monserrato, Italy. She and her colleagues report their findings in an upcoming *Proceedings of the Royal Society of London B: Biology Letters*.

However, Seymour suggests another scenario. He points out that some plants keep the heat on after trapping insects in their chambers, so heat itself might serve as a reward for certain pollinators.

To test that idea, he and his colleagues studied *Cyclocepha colasi* beetles pollinating *Philodendron solimoesense* in French Guiana. As many beetles do, these produce heat to keep their body temperatures high enough for activity. Beetles active in a warm flower during the evening are using less than half the energy they would have used if they had stayed active out in the open, the researchers report in the Nov. 20 *Nature*.

The heat-generating flowers "are like nightclubs for beetles," Seymour says. The warm, alluring environment draws an insect in.

During evolution, a floral innovation may have supplanted the nightclub concept. A flower that offers just a sip of nectar or a pollen snack and then sends the pollinator on its way will probably spread its pollen over many more partners than will a plant that traps insects for a whole night. Seymour's take on why heat rewards died out is that "nightclubs were replaced by fast food."

Web Sites

Due to the changing nature of Internet links, the Rosen Publishing Group, Inc., has developed an online list of Web sites related to the subject of this book. This site is updated regularly. Please use this link to access the list:

http://www.rosenlinks.com/cdfp/lath

For Further Reading

Carter, Ashley. *Classical and Statistical Thermodynamics*. Upper Saddle River, NJ: Prentice Hall, 2000.

Dill, Ken, and Sarina Bromberg. *Molecular Driving Forces: Statistical Thermodynamics in Chemistry and Biology*. New York, NY: Taylor & Francis, Inc., 2002.

Einstein, Albert. *Essays in Science*. New York, NY: Barnes & Noble, 2004.

Gaskell, David, and Robert Rice. *Introduction to the Thermodynamics of Materials*. New York, NY: Taylor & Francis, Inc., 2003.

Highfield, Roger. *The Physics of Christmas: From the Aerodynamics of Reindeer to the Thermodynamics of Turkey*. Boston, MA: Little, Brown and Company, 1999.

McCarthy, Rose. *The Laws of Thermodynamics: Understanding Heat and Energy Transfers* (The Library of Physics). New York, NY: The Rosen Publishing Group, Inc., 2005.

Moran, Michael J., and Howard Shapiro. *Fundamentals of Engineering Thermodynamics*. New York, NY: John Wiley & Sons, Inc., 2003.

Potter, Merle. *Schaum Engineering Thermodynamics.*
New York, NY: The McGraw-Hill Companies, 1997.

Simon, John, and Donald McQuarrie. *Molecular Thermodynamics.* Herndon, VA: University Science Books, 1999.

Taylor, Charles. *The Internal Combustion Engine in Theory and Practice: Volume 1: Thermodynamics, Fluid, Flow, Performance.* Cambridge, MA: MIT Press, 1990.

Van Ness, H. C. *Understanding Thermodynamics.* Mineola, NY: Dover Publications, Inc., 1983.

Bibliography

Barnes, Adam. "Improving Accuracy in Heat Flux Measurements." *Process Heating*, Vol. 8, Issue 10, November 2001, p. 44.

Bejan, Adrian. "How Nature Takes Shape." *Mechanical Engineering-CIME,* Vol. 119, No. 10, October 1997, p. 30.

Bender, Carl M., Dorje C. Brody, and Bernhard K. Meister. "Entropy and Temperature of a Quantum Carnot Engine." *Proceedings of the Royal Society: Mathematical, Physical and Engineering Sciences*, Vol. 458, No. 2022, June 8, 2002, pp. 1519–1526.

Bentley, Mace. "Living with Heat: How Do Residents Cope with the Sweltering Heat and Humidity in Bangkok—Dubbed the Hottest City in the World?" *Weatherwise*, Vol. 57, Issue 1, January/February 2004, p. 16.

Boniface, J. Jay, Ziv Reich, Daniel S. Lyons, and Mark M. Davis. "Thermodynamics of T Cell Receptor Binding to Peptide–MHC: Evidence for a General Mechanism of Molecular Scanning." *Proceedings of the National Academy of Sciences*, Vol. 96, September 1999, pp. 11446–11451.

Callen, Herbert. *Thermodynamics and an Introduction to Thermostatistics*. New York, NY: John Wiley & Sons, 1985.

Fons, Lloyd. "Temperature Anomaly Mapping Identifies Subsurface Hydrocarbons." *World Oil*, September 2000.

Freeman, Ira. *Physics Made Simple*. New York, NY: Doubleday, 1990.

Freudenberger, Bob. "Air Conditioning Theory and Policies." *Auto and Truck International*, Vol. 76, Issue 4, July–August 1999, p. 12.

Gribbon, John, and Mary Gribbon. *Time and Space*. New York, NY: Dorling Kindersley Publishing, Inc., 1994.

Jancovici, Bernard. *Statistical Physics and Thermodynamics*. New York, NY: John Wiley & Sons, 1973.

Jesitus, John. "Energy-Management Systems Provide More Than Savings." *Hotel & Motel Management*, Vol. 216, Issue 11, June 18, 2001, p. 38.

Kenney, J. F., Vladimir A. Kutcherov, Nikolai A. Bendeliani, and Vladimir A. Alekseev. "The Evolution of Multicomponent Systems at High Pressures: VI. The Thermodynamic Stability of the Hydrogen-Carbon System: The Genesis of Hydrocarbons and the Origin of Petroleum." *Proceedings of the National Academy of Sciences*, Vol. 99, No. 17, August 20, 2002, pp. 10976–10981.

Lorenz, Ralph. "Full Steam Ahead—Probably." *Science*, Vol. 299, Issue 5608, February 7, 2003, p. 837.

Lubick, Naomi. "Desert Fridge: Cooling Foods When There's Not a Socket Around." *Scientific American*, November 19, 2000.

Milius, Susan. "Warm-Blooded Plants? OK, There's No Blood, but They Do Make Their Own Heat." *Science News*, Vol. 164, Issue 24, December 13, 2003, p. 379.

Perkins, S. "Clearing Up How Cloud Droplets Freeze— Outside-In." *Science News*, November 30, 2002.

Pinkerton, Frederick E., and Brian G. Wicke. "Bottling the Hydrogen Genie." *The Industrial Physicist*, February/March 2004, pp. 20–23.

Rolexawards.com. "Mohammed Bah Abba." Retrieved November 2004 (http://www.rolexawards.com/ laureates/laureate-6-bah_abba.html).

Segré, Gino. *A Matter of Degrees: What Temperature Reveals About the Past and Future of Our Species, Planet, and Universe*. New York, NY: Penguin Group, 2002.

Soper, Alan K. "Water and Ice." *Science*, Vol. 297, Issue 5585, August 23, 2002, p. 1288.

Voets, Thomas, Guy Droogmans, Ulrich Wissenbach, Annelies Janssens, Veit Flockerzi, and Bernd Nilius. "The Principle of Temperature-Dependent Gating in Cold- and Heat-Sensitive TRP Channels." *Nature*, Vol. 430, August 12, 2004, pp. 748–754.

Voss, David. "Quantum Engine Blasts Past High Gear." *Science*, Vol. 295, Issue 5554, January 18, 2002.

Weiss, Peter. "Another Face of Entropy: Particles Self-Organize to Make Room for Randomness." *Science News*, August 15, 1998.

Weiss, Peter. "Breaking the Law: Can Quantum Mechanics + Thermodynamics = Perpetual Motion?" *Science News*, Vol. 158, No. 15, October 7, 2000.

Index

About the Editor

Jennifer Viegas is a news reporter for the Discovery
Channel and the Australian Broadcasting Corporation.
She also has written for ABC News, *New Scientist*,
Knight-Ridder newspapers, the *Christian Science
Monitor*, the *Princeton Review*, and several other
publications, as well as a number of books for young
adults on a variety of science subjects.

Photo Credits

Front cover (clockwise from top right): "Infinite
Textures" © Comstock Images Royalty-Free Division;
"Boiling Water" © Photo Researchers, Inc.; "Liquid
Crystal" © Getty Images; background image of gyroscope
© Getty Images; portrait, Isaac Newton © Library of
Congress, Prints and Photographs Division. Back
cover: top image "Electrons Orbiting Nucleus" ©
Royalty-Free/Corbis; bottom "Liquid Crystal" © Getty
Images.

Designer: Geri Fletcher; Series Editor: Wayne Anderson